V&R

Manfred Velden

Brain Death of an Idea

The Heritability of Intelligence

With 4 figures

V&R unipress

Bibliographic information published by the Deutsche Nationalbibliothek

The Deutsche Nationalbibliothek lists this publication in the Deutsche Nationalbibliografie;
detailed bibliographic data are available in the Internet at http://dnb.d-nb.de.

ISBN 978-3-8471-0288-5
ISBN 978-3-8470-0288-8 (E-Book)

© Copyright 2014 by V&R unipress GmbH, D-37079 Goettingen

All rights reserved, including those of translation into foreign languages. No part of this work may
be reproduced or utilized in any form or by any means, electronic or mechanical, including
photocopying, microfilm and recording, or by any information storage and retrieval system,
without permission in writing from the publisher.
Printing and binding: ⊕ Hubert & Co, Göttingen

Printed in Germany

Contents

Introduction 7

Part I: The methods for determining the heritability of mental traits, in particular of intelligence 9
    Quantitative genetic studies 9
    Molecular genetic studies 22

Part II: Research on the heritability of intelligence – a dark chapter in the history of science 25
    Galton and the regression effect – a momentous misunderstanding . . 26
    Eugenics – from a plausible idea to paranoia 30
    Immigration and the intelligence of the nation 32
    11^+ – A tragedy unnoticed 34
    Scientific racism 39
    The Eysenck case 44
    Molecular genetic peculiarities 51

Summary and comment 57

Literature 61

Index 65

Introduction

The question as to the degree to which intelligence is heritable appears plausible at first sight and, after many decades of intense research about the topic, we expect a clear answer, particularly because the pertinent science, behavioural genetics, presents itself with many formulae and figures, quite in the style of a natural science. But whoever takes a closer look at the published data and the scientific discussion about the topic will be disappointed.[1] Not only do the published values for the heritability of intelligence range from about 10 % (negligible) to 90 % (higher than the ones for most bodily traits), but the methods used to determine them are utterly contested. Quite a few researchers generally question the soundness of applying methods developed in order to predict breeding success in plants and animals to mental traits (e. g. intelligence) in humans. It must even be asked whether heritability estimates in general are of any scientific or practical worth at all. Attempts to determine the heritability of intelligence by means of molecular genetics, i.e. through an analysis of the DNA[2], a procedure by means of which the solution of the problem has been announced for decades, have yielded no valid indications whatsoever for a genetic aspect of intelligence.[3]

In this situation, anybody interested in the issue cannot but form his own opinion. Without a well founded opinion, he is at the mercy of to a truly chaotic situation characterized by the most diverse and contradictory opinions, claims, deliberations, and data. A well founded opinion, however, requires a close examination of the fundamental premises and principles underlying the procedures by which so-called "heritability coefficients" are being determined. Without a firm grasp of these premises and principles, any idea about the heritability of intelligence (and other mental traits) will remain obscure. In my

---

[1] Popular scientific publications should generally be avoided. They have only contributed to making the discussion more ideological and scientifically obscure.
[2] Desoxyribo Nucleic Acid, giant molecule containing the genetic information.
[3] The molecular genetic procedures used so far are still poorly understood when it comes to interpreting results.

view, the main shortcoming in the debate about the heritability of intelligence, and the cause for the chaotic situation characterizing it, must be seen in the fact that those fundamental premises and principles have rarely, if ever, been made explicit.

In order to avoid that the reader, anticipating what is coming up, closes the book right away, let me stress that the procedures for determining the heritability of intelligence do not require much mathematical skill. The fundamental rules of mathematics will do. Grasping the crux of the matter will not primarily result from mathematically comprehending certain formulae (they are quite simple) but from comprehending the *contextual meaning* of those formulae. This comprehension may not always be simple but, after 30 years of teaching the matter, I am quite confident that my explications will be understandable for anyone seriously interested. Let it be stressed again that without a firm grasp of the methodological basics of the heritability estimates any discussion about the topic must remain totally senseless.

At the end of my explications we will see that there is an obvious discrepancy between what can be said about the topic from a scientific point of view and what is assumed by a broad public and also among many scientists. In my view this discrepancy may only be understood by looking at the history of the discipline dealing with the heritability of mental traits and mental functions, a history going far back into the 19th century. When I say that we are dealing with one of the darkest chapters in the history of science here, both as to the scientific level of the discussion and its social and political repercussions, the reader may anticipate that in this history things have not always been all that scientific. And as we will see, this chapter has in no way been brought to a conclusion. The second and lengthier part of the book is therefore dedicated to it.

Petra Glaubitz deserves my thanks for preparing the figures.

Part I: The methods for determining the heritability of mental traits, in particular of intelligence

There are two approaches by which a determination of the heritability of intelligence may be attempted: the quantitative genetic one, where the heritability is indirectly determined by comparing the resemblance among relatives of different degrees of relatedness, and the molecular genetic one, where, as mentioned, the determination is done by analyzing the DNA. The prevailing notions about the heritability of intelligence, as far as they relate to scientific data in the first place and not just to intuition, all come from quantitative genetic studies. The molecular genetic procedures are still in a kind of testing phase and have, as mentioned, so far not yielded any reliable indications that there is a genetic contribution involved in intelligence. As some scientists are convinced that molecular genetic methods will eventually still reveal a considerable genetic role in the forming of intelligence (a small yet unspecifiable role is assumed by nearly all scientists), those methods as well as their present results will be treated here, too. But first the quantitative genetic methods will be outlined. As we will see the "model" of quantitative genetics implies decisive fundamental assumptions about the relation between genes and environment with regard to their effect on a quantitative trait (intelligence in our case). Knowing these assumptions is indispensable for a coherent discussion of the topic.

Quantitative genetic studies

The methods for determining the heritability of quantitative (continuous) traits (quantitative genetics) were developed in agronomy in the 20s and 30s of the last century in order to render predictions of breeding success possible. Without knowledge about the heritability of a trait (e.g. milk yield in cows) it is impossible to predict how many generations it will take (a crucial economic aspect) before a desired change in that trait is attained.

Quantitative genetics deals with *differences* between individuals. If we all had the same body size, i.e., if there were no differences in body size between people, there would be no point in asking about the heritability of body size. The *extent* to which individuals differ is given in quantitative genetics (and statistics in general) by the so called "variance". In order to compute the variance of a trait measured in a number (n) of individuals, one first computes the mean (M), then the deviation of all the individual values (x_i symbolizes any of these single values) from the mean ($x_i - M$), then the square of all these deviations ($(x_i - M)^2$), then the sum of all these squared deviations ($\Sigma(x_i - M)^2$), and finally the mean of the squared deviations, such that the variance (V) is now defined in the form

$$V = \frac{\Sigma (x_i - M)^2}{n - 1} \quad (1)$$

Why the deviations from the mean are squared, and why n, the number of measured values, is reduced by 1 need not interest us here. Alluding to the described single steps in computing V it is often termed "mean square of deviations". It is obvious that with large differences between single values their deviations from the mean must be large, too, as must therefore be the variance. "Variation" is often used as a synonym for variance. "Standard deviation" in its exact statistical meaning is the square root of the variance.

In quantitative genetics, the concept of variance is of decisive significance because the model of quantitative genetics is one of a partitioning (analysis) of variance, where the variance to be partitioned is the "phenotypic variance" (V_p). The phenotypic variance simply is the variance of a trait (quantitative variable) present and measurable in a population of individuals for whom the heritability of that trait is to be determined.

This phenotypic variance is caused by different factors (often called "sources" of variance). In the simplest of situations there are two causes that create variance: (1) the fact that individuals differ genetically, and (2), the fact that they are raised and live under different environmental conditions. Accordingly the partitioning of the phenotypic variance (V_p) can be written

$$V_p = V_g + V_e \quad (2)$$

where V_g is that part of the phenotypic variance that is caused by genetic differences, V_e the one caused by differences in the environment.[4] In the literature

---

[4] The formula documents the fallacy of the assertion made by the great psychologist and neurotheoretician Donald Hebb that it makes no sense to assign a different weight to genes and environment because genes and environment relate to each other with respect to some behavioural trait as do length and width of a rectangle with respect to its area (Hebb, 1980, p. 72), a view often cited since (e. g. Ehrlich, 2000, p. 6). But the effects of genes and environment

we often find the terms "genetic variance" and "environmental variance" for V_g and V_e. They should be avoided, however, because they may be misleading. V_g is not the genetic variance, i.e. the genetic diversity, but the part of the phenotypic variance which is due to genetic diversity, i.e., to the fact that individuals are genetically different, just as V_e is not the diversity of the individuals' environments, but rather that part of the phenotypic variance which is due to environmental differences. What the genetic and environmental differences creating phenotypic variance actually are, we do not know and need not know for determining some heritability (see below).

The phenotypic variance is further enhanced if genes and environment "interact" with each other in their effect on the trait, interaction being a *statistical* concept here. Let us imagine a specific genetic constellation (out of many possible ones) and a specific environmental constellation (out of many possible ones). Each of these two has a *mean* effect on the phenotypic trait. The mean effect of the genetic constellation is the average of the effects it has in combination with all the existing environmental constellations, and the mean effect of the environmental constellation is the average of the effects it has when combined with all the existing genetic constellations. If the two constellations are combined, i.e. if an individual with its specific genetic outfit happens to exist in a specific environmental setting, it may happen that the two effects on the phenotypic trait simply add up, but it may also happen that the combined effect is larger or smaller than the sum of the two effects. The latter constitutes an interaction effect. If there are such interaction effects (they may of course occur with the most diverse gene/environment combinations) the phenotypic variance is further enhanced and the partitioning of the phenotypic variance must be written

$$V_p = V_g + V_e + V_{ge} \qquad (3)$$

---

on some behavioural trait are additive and not multiplicative, the way width and length of a rectangle are with respect to its area, which is why both may very well have a different weight as to some behavioural trait like intelligence. Length and width of a rectangle are of equal importance as to its area. If, for example, the width or length of a rectangle is reduced by half, the area is reduced by half in both cases, or when length or width is zero, the area is zero, too. With an additive connection, as in the case of the above formula which shows the contribution of genes and environment to the phenotypic variance, the two contributions are independent from each other, such that if V_g were zero, for example, the environmental contribution, V_e, would still be there. Readers may marvel how a well-known psychologist, who dedicates a whole chapter to the gene/environment issue in his famous book "Essay on Mind", can do so in ignorance of quantitative genetics. At the end of the second part of this book they will probably not be that much amazed any more.

where V_{ge} is the portion due to the fact that there are gene/environment interactions.

If individuals are not under experimental control (as they are in agronomy where they can be assigned to environmental conditions at will) a further source of variance may emerge, the so-called gene/environment "covariation". It may be caused by the fact that individuals with a specific genetic constellation actively seek specific environmental conditions or that specific environmental conditions "seek" specific genetic conditions. In the case of intelligence, given that there actually were genetic effects on it, one might imagine that children and youth, who for genetic reasons are more intelligent, would more frequently seek intellectually stimulating environments (like libraries or their electronic analogues), or that parents, teachers, or educators more often hook up with more intelligent children than with less intelligent ones. A situation like that further enhances the variation of a trait such that the partitioning of the phenotypic variance now reads

$$V_p = V_g + V_e + V_{ge} + 2Cov_{ge} \qquad (4)$$

where Cov_{ge} signifies the gene/environment covariation (a form of correlation) and $2Cov_{ge}$ the portion of the phenotypic variance caused by the covariation. The reason why the covariance must be doubled in order to yield the respective variance proportion need not interest us here.

The degree of heritability of a trait is now defined as that part of the phenotypic variance which is caused by genetic differences, and it is given in the form of the so-called "heritability coefficient" (h^2) which is written as

$$h^2 = \frac{V_g}{V_p} \qquad (5)$$

The coefficient is often multiplied by 100, which results in percentage values for heritability[5]. Although it is of no significance for subsequent explications it may, for the sake of completeness, be mentioned that V_g in formula (5) stands for but a part of the genetically caused variance (the so-called "additive genetic variance"), namely the one that determines the resemblance among relatives. As mentioned above, it is by means of this resemblance that the heritability used for predicting breeding success is determined.

---

5 Previously h (for heritability) was the symbol for the heritability coefficient. At that time, it was defined as a ratio of *standard deviations*, which, as mentioned, are the square roots of the variances. So when changing to variances h had to be squared.

Formula (5) is just the *definition* of heritability. We cannot measure V_g, just infer it, namely from the resemblance among relatives. Evidently the resemblance with respect to some trait among relatives of different degrees of relatedness tells us something about the heritability of that trait. If a trait is heritable to some degree, siblings, for example, must resemble each other to a higher degree than half siblings because siblings have 50 % of the genes in common, while half siblings only share 25 %. In this sense, identical (monozygotic) twins and fraternal (dizygotic) twins are of different degrees of relatedness because the monozygotic share 100 % of the genes while the dizygotic share only 50 %, quite like normal siblings. A typical computational formula for determining heritability on the basis of resemblance is

$$h^2 = 2(t_{MZ} - t_{DZ}) \qquad (6)$$

where t_{MZ} is the resemblance of the monozygotic twins, and t_{DZ} the one for the dizygotic twins.[6] In order to avoid some misunderstanding let it be stressed that resemblance is meant as the one *with respect to the trait* (body size, intelligence) and not resemblance in the common sense of looking alike. There is a standard procedure for determining resemblance in quantitative genetics, of course, the so-called intraclass correlation, a procedure analogous to the common (product moment) correlation, which provides values between zero and unity.[7]

A question which has taken ample space in the controversy about the heritability of intelligence must be addressed, namely the question of whether methods developed in order to predict breeding success with respect to bodily traits in animals may be meaningfully applied to mental traits in humans. As mentioned at the outset, the question is being answered in the negative by many researchers. It shall nevertheless be dealt with here briefly even though heritability coefficients for mental traits in humans do not make any sense, neither scientifically nor practically, even if the above question were answered in the affirmative (see below). A short deliberation about the validity of heritability coefficients may already make sense at this point insofar as it may give an idea of the way in which, in this field of research about the heritability of intelligence,

---

6 It is recommended that the reader not reason further about why this is so, because he probably misses an exact definition of t, as well as a number of mental steps that lead up to the formula. It is evident, however, that the larger the difference in resemblance between the two types of twins, the greater the heritability.
7 The difference between the two procedures as well as the necessity to develop a specific procedure for determining the resemblance among relatives need not be discussed here because they are not necessary for understanding the further discourse.

methods and data have come to be dealt with. This aspect is of primary concern in the second part of the book.

Let us first address the validity of heritability coefficients stemming from *agronomic* studies in which, different from studies with humans, things are under experimental control and where, for example, assignment of individuals to environmental conditions is possible. This will show that among those who do the methodologically much more problematic studies about mental traits in humans, quite unrealistic opinions as to the validity of their results have evolved.

Ronald Fisher, one of the creators of quantitative genetics, already took a critical view of what heritability coefficients can tell us. He spoke of the "...so called coefficient of heritability which I regard as one of those unfortunate shortcuts which have emerged in biometry for lack of a more thorough analysis of the data." (Fisher, 1951, p. 217). Falconer, author of the essential introduction to quantitative genetics, writes about heritability determinations in animals and plants in general, "Heritability cannot easily be estimated with any great precision, and most estimates have rather large standard errors." (Falconer & Mackay, 1996, p. 161). He then cites some heritability values that have been computed for bodily traits in humans and animals (cattle, pigs, poultry, mice, drosophila melanogaster (fruit fly)) which, on average, are about 40 %, with a standard error (square root of the variance) of 2 to 4 %. For twin studies, which are seen as yielding particularly valid results by some, he gives the above computation formula (formula (6)), yet points out that this kind of heritability estimate critically rests on several assumptions, among others that the environmentally caused variance is the same for both kinds of twins. Among a large number of reasons why even this precondition will *not* be satisfied, he lists just seven, the presence of which mostly cannot be tested (e.g. the competition in utero being the same for both kinds of twins). The explicitness and resoluteness with which Falconer addresses these problems alone should keep a scientist who takes scientific rigor seriously from conducting a twin study. This notwithstanding, Falconer presents data from such a study (not conducted by himself) that yielded a heritability of 66 % for body size and of 34 % for intelligence in humans (Falconer & Mackay, 1996, p. 173).

Comparing these data given by Falconer with the heritability values for intelligence as presented by psychologists, one cannot help but notice a large discrepancy. Even if we ignore Eysenck's (1998) value of 80 % (reasons for ignoring Eysenck's data in general are given in the second part of the book), we still find values for late adolescence (the values for children are smaller) of 75 % (Neisser et al., 1996) or "somewhere" between 40 and 80 % (Nisbett et al., 2012). These values are not only much higher than the ones given by Falconer for intelligence but even higher than the ones he gives for bodily traits in animals, although these are based on experimental studies and thus particularly valid.

As mentioned quite a few critics have denied that the methods of quantitative genetics may be meaningfully applied to mental traits in humans (e.g. Bailey, 1997; Hirsch, 1990; Kempthorne, 1978, 1997; Layzer, 1974; Lewontin, 1975; Platt & Bach, 1997; Schönemann, 1997; Schwartz & Schwartz, 1973; Wahlsten, 1990) and have assumed that the data published are overestimations of an unspecifiable degree. Let us take as an example one of the most often cited twin studies, the one by Tellegen et al. (1988). The authors report to have used the formula given (and extensively criticized, see above) by Falconer

$$h^2 = 2(t_{MZ} - t_{DZ}) \qquad (6)$$

They do so not only without saying one word about why they think the preconditions for its use were met, but also without mentioning that there might be any methodological problems with applying the formula in the first place. Looking at the formula it is easy to see that an overestimation of the resemblance of the monozygotic twins (t_{MZ}) by an amount of just .1 (the t-values may range from zero to one), results in an overestimation of heritability by an amount of 20 %, which may easily happen due to a smaller environmentally caused variance in the monozygotic twins.

All this may suffice for the reader to gain an impression about the questionable validity of heritability coefficients in general, and those for intelligence in particular, and to demonstrate that in the research field about the heritability of intelligence peculiar standards have developed as far as the use of methods and data in it.

However that may be, it is possible to circumvent the whole discussion about the validity of heritability coefficients for intelligence altogether by addressing two fundamental questions: (1) can there possibly be a general value for the heritability of intelligence, even if the above mentioned validity problems were solved (which they are not and will not be)?; and again, given that solution, (2) what might be the sense of determining those coefficients in the first place?

As these questions, which should be asked at the beginning of any discourse about the topic, are usually not asked at all, we might assume that they are generally seen as having already been answered. But, in fact, they have rarely if ever been asked at all in the long tradition of contemplating the heritability of intelligence since the 19th century. Most probably it has been taken for granted that the heritability of intelligence is a natural constant (which would answer question (1)) and also that it reveals to what degree intelligence is malleable (which would answer question (2)). In addition, answering these questions may cast doubt on more than 100 years of research (and a whole field of research), a prospect that may have prompted researchers in the field, consciously or unconsciously, not to ask them in the first place. Interestingly, the questions are rather easy to answer and the answers in no way confirm the above mentioned implicit assumptions.

As to the first question: can there be *one* binding heritability coefficient for intelligence, or at least one for a limited number of specific, defined populations?

The first part of the question can be answered in a straightforward way when, in the formula that defines the heritability coefficient

$$h^2 = \frac{V_g}{V_p} \qquad (5)$$

we break the phenotypic variance into its constituent parts (formula (4)), such that

$$h^2 = \frac{V_g}{V_g + V_e + V_{ge} + 2Cov_{ge}} \qquad (7)$$

If there is to be a universally binding value for the heritability of intelligence or just a rather narrow range of values (such values and ranges have been presented time and again), the terms on the right side of the equation must be constants, i.e. they would have to be identical for all the populations on earth one may think of. We may actually assume this to be so for V_g because the human species (homo sapiens) may be seen as genetically rather homogeneous (e.g. Bodmer & Cavalli-Sforza, 1976; Rogers & Jorde, 1995), particularly considering that the obvious genetic differences which make people look so different in Africa, Europe, or Asia are irrelevant in the context of the heritability of intelligence. So V_g, if not a constant, will differ little between different populations on earth. But may sameness everywhere on earth also be assumed for the other terms? Just considering V_e, one immediately recognizes that this can in no way be assumed. The environmental differences which determine V_e may considerably differ in size for different populations. Even though we in no way know in detail which environmental factors are relevant for the shaping of intelligence, psychologists still have specified some of these factors, factors of which we know that they play an important part without us being able to numerically determine the degree to which they do. Neisser et al. (1996), in their report on the situation of intelligence research put together in the aftermath of the turmoil about the book "The Bell Curve" by Herrnstein and Murray (1994, see below), for example, list the factors "schooling" and "family environment". Clearly school quality, socioeconomic status, or educational level of families vary to quite different degrees in different populations. If we just consider differences between countries there are those in which all children go to comparably good schools (we may, for example, think of the traditionally egalitarian Scandinavian countries), and those in which a small minority go to good schools while the majority go to bad schools and a not all that small minority do not go to school at all because they must work or because there simply are no schools for them (we may, for example, think of certain developing countries). The same holds for differences in socio-economic status or educational background of families.

As to the terms V_{ge} and Cov_{ge}, we cannot make any assumptions whatsoever about the conditions under which specific gene/environment interactions or covariations may occur. We may assume, however, that with an increase in V_e there will be a tendency for V_{ge} and Cov_{ge} to increase, too, because a larger number of environmental conditions allows for a larger number of gene/environment combinations (and thus a larger number of interaction effects) as well as a larger degree of gene/environment covariation. By contrast, neither interactions nor covariation would be possible in the case of just one environmental condition (no environmental differences).

After what has been said, it should be clear that, in contrast to what has been asserted time and again, there can be no general value or even half-way narrow range of values for the heritability of intelligence. Even the claim that there is a "high degree of heritability for intelligence" is wrong, because, depending on environmental conditions, the heritability of intelligence may be quite low. Atkinson et al. (1993) report published values between 10 and 87 %, Scarr (1974) such between zero and 90 %, and Nisbett et al. (2012) even write "…heritability can take practically any value for any trait…" or "…the heritability of intelligence is between zero and one…" (p. 132). In addition to the different degrees to which the conditions for applying quantitative genetics are not satisfied, the large differences in environmentally caused variance components between the populations studied are probably the main cause of the extraordinary diversity of heritability estimates. Due to the above mentioned relative genetic homogeneity of homo sapiens, the diversity of *genetically* caused variance components between populations should be comparably small and only marginally involved in causing the large differences in reported heritability coefficients. These extreme differences in heritability coefficients, as well as their cause, have all too rarely been pointed out in the literature (Scarr, 1974; Velden, 1997, 2003, 2010; Nisbett et al., 2012), which has resulted in the spreading of the totally false impression of a generally high degree of heritability of intelligence.

Now how about different heritability estimates *for specific populations?* With respect to the relevant factors in shaping intelligence, like school quality or family environment, we must not only expect large differences in environmentally caused variance components between countries or states, but also, and maybe even to a higher degree, between regions or cities within these countries, and between districts or quarters within regions or cities. In so far there is such a great number of subpopulations for which heritability estimates would have to be performed that the whole endeavour would be impractical due to the very lack of a sufficient number of twin pairs. In addition there are simply no sufficiently clear criteria on the basis of which one could assume the homogeneous environmental variation necessary for a meaningful heritability coefficient. When contemplating these problems a little, we soon discover that a list of valid heritability coefficients for specific populations is an odd idea. All that can be said about the heritability of intelligence, even if it is for once assumed that quantitative genetics may be meaningfully applied to mental traits in humans (which it may not), is that the values may be extremely different, with the ranges given by Scarr (zero to 90 %), Atkinson et al. (10 to 87 %) or Nisbett et al. (zero to 100 %) appearing quite realistic. *The* heritability of intelligence is therefore pure fiction.

Let us now address the second one of the two questions posed above: What might be the objective of, or sense in determining heritability coefficients for intelligence? It not possibly being the objective for which heritabilities are determined in agronomy, namely the prediction of breeding success, one should assume that the question must have been discussed somewhere. This, however, not being the case, we must assume that the scientists who have performed those laborious estimates took the sense of what they were doing for granted or – not even this should be ruled out – simply did not much think about the question.

As mentioned above, it has probably been assumed, implicitly or explicitly, that heritability coefficients for intelligence allow us to predict to what degree this trait can be enhanced by qualified intervention. The assumption was explicitly addressed in Jensen's famous/notorious article of 1969, in which he argued that intervention programs for minorities in the USA must remain ineffective because, due to its high heritability, intelligence may be enhanced to a minimal degree only.[8] I cannot discern what further purpose, other than that of evaluating such intervention programs, heritability estimates for intelligence might possibly have. The idea of in the long run enhancing intelligence by manipulating the DNA (about the molecular genetic basis of intelligence, see below) I deem scientifically so utopian and so questionable morally that I do not believe that serious scientists really do think along these lines.

What about the scientific basis of the assumption, so plausible sounding though, that intelligence can be the less changed by social intervention the more heritable it is? This assumption probably appears plausible to us because our notions about the relation between heritability and malleability of traits have

---

8 More about Jensen's article as well as its further implications, particularly in connection with eugenics, will be found in the second part of the book.

been shaped by our knowledge about the heritability of bodily traits, often qualitative ones like eye or hair colour, and about genetic diseases. Bodily traits can usually only be altered to a limited degree, and mutations often cause diseases which, all progress in medicine notwithstanding, are to this day not curable. However, with quantitative mental traits like intelligence, which to a high degree are susceptible to socio-cultural effects, things are completely different. Their heritability is determined, as we have seen, by means of a statistical instrument (quantitative genetics), and in statistics, as many of us have experienced, we often find quite logical, yet at the same time implausible ("counterintuitive") conclusions.

The first counterintuitive conclusion we meet upon dealing with the heritability/malleability issue is, as we have seen above, that heritability is a function of the environment. If we once again look at the definition of heritability in the form

$$h^2 = \frac{V_g}{V_g + V_e + V_{ge} + 2Cov_{ge}} \qquad (7)$$

it is immediately obvious that the heritability is the larger the smaller the environmentally determined or codetermined variance components are, because these are part of the denominator. An egalitarian society which, in order to create equal educational opportunities for all, tries to keep the environmentally determined variance components small will automatically, yet not by intent, bring about an increase in heritability. As mentioned, the large differences between heritabilities reported – the coefficients cover the whole range of possible values – must, in light of the high genetic homogeneity of homo sapiens, be primarily caused by the large differences between societies with respect to the environmental factors shaping intelligence. For genetically identical populations there can therefore be quite different heritabilities. A high heritability coefficient is thus largely not caused by a high genetically determined variance component but by a small environmentally determined one. In order to illustrate these facts and to elucidate their relevance for the relation between heritability and malleability, let us imagine two scenarios. In the first one, we are dealing with two children who have problems in school due to their insufficient mental capacity. One of them lives in an egalitarian society with generally small differences in educational opportunities, in which the heritability of intelligence therefore is quite high. The second one lives in a developing country with large differences as to the environmental factors relevant for the development of intelligence, in which its heritability is accordingly quite low. Are the possibilities for helping the first child now reduced, due to the high heritability in its population, by comparison to the chances of helping the second child? Quite obviously this is not so because this assumption would lead us to the absurd conclusion that the chances for the first child could be enhanced by moving to a developing country with it and having it treated there. The success of interventions depends solely on the specific problems of the children and on the quality of the intervention measures addressing those problems. The heritability in the respective populations is irrelevant for the success of those interventions. In the second scenario we are dealing with an ideally egalitarian society in which the heritability of intelligence is therefore close to 100 %. In such a society, too, there may be problems in school for individual children (e. g. due to personal problems in the relation between the children and their parents or between teachers and their pupils) even though they occur quite rarely, which is why the heritability coefficient in this population is only minimally affected by those cases. Is there now no help possible for a child with problems in this society as the near 100 % heritability of intelligence might suggest? Clearly the conclusion is nonsensical. The heritability of intelligence in a population is largely determined by the environmental differences effective on average in this population, which in our scenario happen to be small. But just as there can be detrimental environmental conditions for single individuals or groups of individuals there may be forms of intervention designed for those individuals or groups which are highly effective. The environmental differences effective on average in a given population, and largely determining the heritability coefficient, cannot tell anything about the effectiveness of intervention measures specifically designed to help disadvantaged children because those environmental differences and the intervention measures are independent of each other. So the effectiveness of intervention measures is in no way constrained by the fact that the environmental differences in the population happen to be small.

In the aftermath of Jensen's 1969 article in which he doubted the potential for improving the mental capacity of minorities on account of the high heritability of intelligence, one has repeatedly pointed to the fact that a high heritability does not imply unchangeability (e. g. Neisser et al., 1996). The statement is true but can be misleading if it is not further elaborated. It may be understood as meaning that the heritability actually puts limits to malleability but that there is always at least some leeway for change. But it is crucial to keep in mind that with human intelligence a heritability coefficient tells practically nothing about malleability at all.

Once again inspecting formula (7) it must be clear that h^2 cannot really be zero because V_g, according to almost all scientists, is not zero, however small it may be in relation to the environmentally caused variance components. So may we imagine a human population in which V_g is so large that it actually reduces the degree of malleability to a relevant degree? For that to happen we might imagine, even though not without some degree of fantasy, a hypothetical population, in which "human" is to be understood as having evolved from members of the genus "homo". That would require, however, that extinct members of the genus homo, like, for example, homo erectus, homo heidelbergensis, or homo neanderthalensis, had survived and had been capable of reproducing with homo sapiens. For those extinct species we may assume that the biological basis for acquiring language was less well developed than that of homo sapiens, such that mixing with homo sapiens would have created a population quite inhomogeneous as to the neural substrate of language acquisition. In this case there would have been major genetic differences between individuals as to their capacity to develop intelligence, and thus a genetically determined variance component not insignificant as compared to the environmentally determined ones. As a consequence the possibility to change the mental capacity by means of social intervention would be substantially reduced. The emergence of such an inhomogeneous species would not only have been unlikely biologically, but even more so sociologically, however. Reviewing the history of the relations between the diverse ethnic groups *within* homo sapiens we should be glad that, except for homo sapiens, the last forms of the genus homo went extinct long before our time. Homogeneity may not be that much worth striving for, yet in the case of the genetic homogeneity of our species with respect to developing intelligence we are clearly dealing with a stroke of luck. It allows us, if scientific reason eventually prevails in this ill-fated field, to deposit the idea of genetically based mental differences between ethnic groups in the archive for particularly dangerous misconceptions.

Looking back, let me summarize the most important insights about the endeavor to determine the heritability of intelligence:

1. It is contested whether quantitative genetics may be meaningfully applied to mental traits in humans.
2. There cannot possibly exist a general heritability coefficient or just a fairly narrow range of heritability coefficients for intelligence. The values computed nearly cover the whole range from zero to 100 %.
3. A heritability coefficient tells us practically nothing about the possibilities of changing intelligence through social intervention.

The last two aspects alone allow a definite verdict about the field of research dealing with heritability estimates for intelligence: they do not make any sense, neither scientifically nor practically.

Molecular genetic studies

Quantitative genetics attempts to determine the heritability of traits *indirectly* (by comparing the resemblance of relatives of different degrees of relatedness) and even the most optimistic researchers in the field have been conscious of the fact that this kind of heritability determination, particularly when applied to mental traits like intelligence, is not as valid as one wishes it to be. It has therefore been announced for a long time that the problem of the heritability of intelligence will sooner or later be solved in a *direct* way, i.e. via an inspection of the DNA, a solution that one may then consider as the definite one as the immediate material basis of the heritability of intelligence would have been found. The hope for this solution has been enhanced dramatically through the swift progress in genetics, in particular, the development of ever faster and less expensive methods for reading the genetic code.

The first attempt to determine the heritability of intelligence by way of molecular genetics was made by Robert Plomin, who claimed to have demonstrated a high degree of heritability for intelligence by means of twin studies and had predicted the molecular genetic proof for decades.

The procedure of molecular genetic heritability estimates uses so-called SNPs (single nucleotide polymorphisms). The DNA is composed of basic molecules called nucleotides which are all identical except that they may contain four different nitrogen bases: adenine, guanine, cytosine and thymine (therefore the term "polymorphisms"). The sequence of the bases on the DNA constitutes the genetic code for the synthesis of proteins. Proteins partake in the shaping of bodily traits which, for their part, can influence psychological traits. Psychological traits (like intelligence) are abstractions (so-called "constructs"), which in psychology are defined and measured through behaviour. In so far there can be no genes for psychological traits, just ones that have an effect on psychological traits and functions through the production of proteins.

The molecular genetic procedure for determining the heritability of intelligence consists in finding a statistical relation between base sequences and the performance in a test of intelligence. From the strength of the relation, the proportion of the variance of test intelligence that is caused by differences in base sequences can be determined. Plomin's study yielded a proportion of .004, i.e., of .4 % (Zimmer, 2008). This value must be a clear underestimation, however, because for body size, for which there are rather valid quantitative genetic estimates (according to Falconer a heritability of 66 %, Falconer & Mackay, 1996, p. 173), the same procedure only yielded a little more than 5 % variance explained by base sequence differences. But if the underestimation in the case of intelligence were of the same order of magnitude as with body size we still would have to expect a heritability of well below 10 %. However that may be, the molecular genetic heritability estimates are still in a kind of testing phase and we have to wait for further development in this field. Thus a statistically not yet analyzed Chinese study is aiming to find a genetic basis of very high intelligence by genetically comparing a group of highly gifted subjects with a group of normal ones, while Plomin, using data from the same study, has been aiming to find genes that connect to intelligence in general (Yong, 2013). So far, however, all studies conducted after the one mentioned above failed to find any valid indications for intelligence being heritable to a substantial degree. The figures for variance explained reported by Plomin et al. (2012) are all below 1 % (p. 207, 208). Accordingly, the chances for success of the above study with highly gifted subjects are seen as rather small by most scientists (Yong, 2013).

As mentioned, behavioural geneticists hope for a final answer to the question about the heritability of intelligence by means of molecular genetics. It is crucial, however, at this point to keep in mind that for heritability estimates from molecular genetics the same applies as what has been said above for those from quantitative genetics: (1) a value is only valid for the population in which it was determined and may be quite different for other populations due to different environmentally determined variance components and (2) it does not tell anything about the degree to which the trait may be changed through social intervention. If it were actually found that differences in SNP sequences in certain parts of the DNA relate to differences in test intelligence, this would only indicate that genes somehow participate in shaping intelligence. The amount of phenotypic variance, i.e. the differences in intelligence as measured, of course still depends on environmental differences, too, and, considering the vast environmental differences existing and the high genetic homogeneity of homo sapiens, it does so to a higher degree than it does on genetic differences. A molecular genetic heritability value, if it were actually found and replicated, would only show that there is, in principle, a genetic contribution to intelligence. In so far it must be asked what sense there is in determinig molecular genetic heritability estimates for psychological traits. If they actually did show a certain degree of heritability of such a trait, we would not be smarter than we were before. That there is some yet undeterminable degree of heritability of intelligence is not denied by anyone anyway. If a certain degree of heritability were to be determined for some population, it could not be generalized because it would still largely depend on the degree of environmental variation and tell as little about the malleability of intelligence as does one determined by means of quantitative genetics. Some researchers may think, yet not speak, of using molecular genetic studies of intelligence in order to be capable in the long run of enhancing intelligence through manipulations of the DNA. To me this is both, scientifically and technologically utopian, and ethically questionable.[9]

Under these circumstances, it seems requisite to finally diagnose brain death for the research field dealing with the heritability of intelligence and to stop the life saving flow of money into it.

---

9 That notwithstanding, an improvement through social intervention must be more efficient anyway due to the dominant role of the environment in forming intelligence.

Part II: Research on the heritability of intelligence – a dark chapter in the history of science

Presenting the historical background does not serve academic completeness here but is necessary for understanding today's situation in this seemingly unending heritability discussion in which the scientific-methodological facts, as presented in the first part of this book, have been largely ignored and the impression prevails that intelligence is heritable to a large degree and that this is of high theoretical and practical significance. Ironically this impression prevails in a broader public, not because it has been falsely and crudely (mis-) informed by science journalists, but because it also prevails among many scientists whose assertions the journalists refer to.[10] Of course false assumptions or even prejudices that affected the way things were seen have always existed in science. Since Thomas Kuhn's "The Structure of Scientific Revolutions" (1962), everybody who has dealt a little with the history and philosophy of science knows that science is embedded in a social and ideational process which is not necessarily oriented toward purely scientific principles and, as a consequence, in no way leads to continuous scientific progress.[11] But clearly there have been unambiguous and great scientific achievements. In the natural sciences in particular, but not only there, scientific principles, like empiricism, objectivity, and logic, turned out to be effective correctives which ultimately enforced progress toward the truth. By contrast, and beginning with Galton and having to this day not ended, the field of research about the heritability of intelligence, which presents itself quite in the fashion of a natural science, is characterized by the fact that those correctives are largely absent. The topic is as contested today as it ever was and anyone who has some prescientific opinion about the matter may just search around a little in the scientific literature and will soon be able to

---

10 The responsibility lies with the scientists, of course, and not with the journalists because the former should know better.
11 In medicine in particular progress has repeatedly been hampered by a "dominant expert opinion".

underpin his opinion as a scientifically founded one with quotes from that literature.

In order to understand how this actually chaotic scientific situation could come about (and eventually perhaps find a way out of it), it is important for someone who starts to deal with the topic to recognize as early as possible that in this area of research peculiar criteria have evolved about what has to be regarded as correct. In a science that merits to be called one, we expect, after decades of intensive research, progress in terms of generally accepted results. If, as in the case of research about the heritability of intelligence, after more than 100 years of research, anybody may opine about the issue just as he likes, this can only be due to the peculiar criteria used in this research, i. e., to an inappropriate scientific approach in general. In order to get an idea, a feeling if you wish, of that approach, and the attitude that comes with it, of the scientific mindset characteristic of this research area, so to speak, it is helpful to inspect its history, i. e. its origin and the course along which the principles of the approach, those peculiar criteria, have evolved.

Let us begin with the beginning, the start, which was a false start right away, though this metaphor is somewhat inappropriate insofar as in sports a false start is generally recognized as such and a new and correct one arranged, while the start of the research about the heritability of intelligence was seen as a brilliant achievement at the time, and still is today by some scientists. It is particularly interesting to look at why the false start was not recognized as such.

Galton and the regression effect – a momentous misunderstanding

The idea that mental traits, quite like bodily ones, are heritable, has not been developed by science but is probably as old as mankind. Remarks like "This stubbornness he inherited from his grandfather" or "Her aunt was such a musical talent, too" have always been around. The scientific treatment of the topic started with that preexisting firm belief, and the conviction that mental traits are heritable was so firm, even unshakable, that it appeared to be scientifically confirmed time and again, even if data and facts did not tell anything about that heritability at all.

The study of the topic in the narrow sense of a science, which requires measurement techniques for mental traits as well as statistical procedures, begins with Galton, a cousin of Darwin's. Due to his manifold contributions to science, to statistics and inheritance in particular, he is seen by many as a giant in mental history, hardly of lesser importance than his still more famous cousin. Admired greats of intellectual history usually have accomplished great things, of course, but their elevation into the Olympus has not rarely had its downside in that critics have often not dared to speak out, which is understandable given they were dealing with gods. In this way Aristotle, for example, rather more hindered than helped progress in physics with his writings. Let us therefore view Galton not as hovering in the clouds of Olympus but as a common mortal who touched the earth with his feet.

As such he was sent to Cambridge by his wealthy father in order to study medicine, and, at his own request, mathematics. In mathematics he did not excel but looked admiringly at those who did (Richards, 1987, p. 170). He finally managed to get a bachelor's degree (A.B., artium baccalaureus) after which he carried on with his medical studies, which he gave up, however, having earned poor grades in medicine in his A.B. exam. As Richards (1987) comments on Galton's achievements at university and his later near obsessive dealing with genius as an inherited capacity "For one who had failed to achieve eminence at university, the doctrine that genius had biological roots and could not be earned in schoolboy labor must have had an appeal" (p. 171). His interest in mathematics endured in the form of an interest in statistics, however. It eventually led him to find the regression effect. This is generally seen as a great scientific achievement accomplished in combination with his later dominant interest, the study of inheritance.

When comparing the body size of parents with that of their children, he found out that the values of the children had a tendency to be closer to the mean of the children than the values of the parents were in relation to the mean of the parents (Galton, 1886). This effect he called "regression (from Latin regredi, to walk back) towards mediocrity", later "regression toward the mean", simply called "regression" in statistics later on. There was a *tendency* for the values of the children to lie closer to the mean, meaning that at times they could lie further away from the mean. Having found the effect in connection with his studies of inheritance, and probably because his attention was largely occupied by the heritability issue, he deemed it to be a law of inheritance, and it is exactly this which constitutes the above mentioned false start of statistical heritability research.[12] Galton's assumption was so extremely consequential (and, as we will see, still is today) because now there seemed to be a mathematically formulizable law (which is about the most beautiful thing that can happen in science) that described the heritability of quantitative traits.

In order to recognize Galton's misapprehension one must call to mind the fundamental concepts of correlation and regression statistics (developed long after Galton). Correlation and regression statistics deals with associations between variables, yet not with the "perfect" forms of relatedness we find in mathematics and large parts of physics which are described by equations which

---

12 The necessary new start came, yet only decades later, in the form of quantitative genetics.

allow us, given a value on one of the variables, to determine the exact value for the other one.

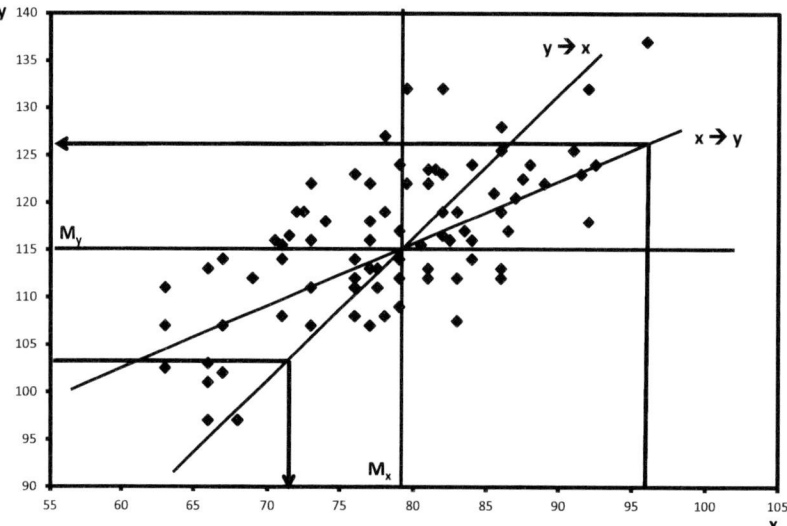

Figure 1. Statistical relation between two variables (x and y).

In statistics, when making deductions from one variable to the other, the term "predict" is often used. Statistical associations are ones of tendency only and do not allow exact predictions. Figure 1 depicts such an association, a so-called "correlation", which has an exact statistical definition. The values indicating the strength of the association, mostly symbolized by r, may vary between -1 and +1, where negative values indicate an inverse relation. The relation depicted in figure 1 constitutes a correlation of the size +.61. Under such conditions one can obviously not make exact inferences from one variable to the other. In order to still make inferences, inexact ones though with a minimum amount of error,[13] regression statistics has been developed. The inferences are made via so-called "regression lines", of which there are, as we can see from figure 1, two, one to infer (predict) from x to y ($x \rightarrow y$), the other one to infer from y to x ($y \rightarrow x$). In figure 1 two such inferences are shown, one from $x = 96$ via the line $x \rightarrow y$ to $y = 127$, the other from $y = 104$ via $y \rightarrow x$ to $x = 72$. It can clearly be seen that in both cases the inferred values are closer to the mean than the ones from which the inference was made. This constitutes the regression effect.

The rationale described so far is in perfect analogy to what Galton found when

---

13 "minimum amount of error" means that the mean square (see above) of the deviations of the predicted values from the actual ones is minimal.

comparing the body size of parents with the one of their children, on which occasion he found the regression effect and gave it its name.[14] This is still today seen as a great scientific achievement and rightfully so. Galton's misapprehension, prompted by the fact that he knew about regression exclusively from inheritance studies, was his assumption that he was dealing with a biological law of inheritance. He did not discern (and probably could not under his circumstances) the generality of the effect which can be inferred from it occurring with any correlational (i. e. not mathematical-functional) relation between variables, irrespective of whether they are of a biological nature or not. Galton's preoccupation with inheritance which induced him to try to predict the body size of children from that of their parents, probably kept him from realizing the above described fact that the regression occurs in both directions of inference, in other words, that when the values of parents are inferred from those of their children, the same effect occurs as when drawing conclusions about the children from the parents.[15]

Mistaking the regression effect for a biological law rather automatically leads to ignoring the fact that the parent-child regression effect is determined genetically *and* environmentally, because the environment naturally codetermines the parent-child correlation and thus the parent-child regression (the higher the correlation the smaller the regression effect). That all this needs to be stressed to this day, the example below of the great psychologist and heritability researcher Hans Jürgen Eysenck will render obvious. More than 100 years after Galton and all the way to his last book, he still deemed the parent-child regression effect to be a biological law.

With respect to psychology, Galton came to be both interesting and relevant thanks to his studies and notions about the heritability of *mental* traits, for which he, even more than for bodily traits, assumed a high or even exclusive dominance of inheritance. In one of his best known books, "Hereditary Genius" (1869), in which he meticulously documents the disproportionate occurrence of "ingenious" judges, statesmen, literary men, men of science etc. in certain families, the common family background is not even mentioned as an environmental factor. In the "Prefatory Chapter" of the second edition (1892), he explicitly writes: "… ability does not exclude the effects of education, which genius does." (p. VIII). At least it is shown by the quote that Galton did occa-

---

14 The body size of the children had a tendency to lie closer to the mean of the children than the one of the parents were in relation to the mean of the parents, and this effect was the stronger the more the body size values of the parents differed from the parents' mean.

15 We are dealing with a seeming paradox here, not rarely found in statistics. Without questioning the reader's logical capabilities let me stress, that the above does *not* mean, that the children's values generally lie closer to the mean than those of the parents and that at the same time those of the parents lie geneneraly closer to the mean than those of the children.

sionally think about environmental effects in the context of mental traits, which one may at times doubt when reading his elaborations.

Eugenics – from a plausible idea to paranoia

Galton's assumptions about the heritability of mental traits, largely unfounded scientifically, had enormous social consequences, particularly in the form of legislations. In discussing these consequences, emphasis should be laid less on their detailed description and more on the degree of scientific cluelessness prompting these consequences.

When Galton, inspecting demographic data that showed a particularly numerous offspring in the English underclass, drew the connection to evolution theory, a frightening idea befell him, which Darwin eventually phrased like this: "Thus the reckless, degraded, and often vicious members of society tend to increase at a quicker rate than the provident and generally virtuous members." (Darwin, 2004/1879, p. 164). This, so Darwin thought, must create a "downward tendency" with respect to the moral values of society. While Darwin could yet imagine some mechanisms countering that trend, for example that the reckless must suffer from a higher mortality, Galton was really alarmed, so much so that he founded the eugenics movement which was to effect the regulation of marriage and family size in accordance with the genetic constitution of the parents.[16] As to the practical application of the idea starting soon afterwards, it should be mentioned that Galton did not have any compulsory measures in mind.

Galton and Darwin were not aware of the dangers of the eugenic idea. Specifically they could not imagine that a *state*, not just some morally perverse intellectuals, would make a program of mass murder of the handicapped out of it, as eventually happened in Nazi Germany.

As indicated by Darwin's quote, the eugenics movement mainly alluded to *mental* traits. In the end it was intelligence again that would play the decisive role, as a trait of course assumed to be to a large degree heritable, since otherwise the eugenic idea would not have made any sense.

Even though in no way comparable to the crimes of the Third Reich, the eugenic idea, which in many countries and within a few years mutated into paranoid apprehensions about an intellectual/moral decline, soon had morally questionable consequences, too. Today, we are irritated and look in disbelief upon the fact that those consequences came to pass in *democratic* societies.

---

16 The term eugenics, coined by Galton in 1883, derives from Greek "well –born". Galton is seen as the founder of the movement, while its most influential proponent and theoretician was Charles Davenport (e.g. Davenport, 1911)

As early as 1907, just a few years after the eugenic idea had begun to spread, the US state of Indiana passed the first law about compulsory sterilisation in history. As Lombardo (2011) writes: "In time more than 30 states and a dozen foreign countries followed Indiana's lead in passing sterilization laws; those and other laws restricting immigration and regulating marriage on "eugenic" grounds were still in effect in the United States as late as the 1970s." (p. IX).

In today's view, compulsory sterilization, even if the consent of kin is required as by Minnesota's sterilization law passed in 1925, is felt as repulsive and seen as unacceptable. But there were no sinister machinations, unnoticed by a wider public, behind those laws. Rather, it is our system of values, particularly of those concerning individual rights, that has changed profoundly since then. This becomes quite obvious by what Oliver Wendell Holmes, justice at the Supreme Court and highly respected still today, said about the Court's 1927 upholding of the constitutionality of compulsory sterilization: "Three generations of imbeciles are enough." (Holmes, 1935). Today, such a remark would be viewed as intolerable in the whole political spectrum, except for the extreme right.

Oliver Wendell Holmes' remark points to the dominant role intelligence played in compulsory sterilization. Indiana's law referred to criminals, the feebleminded, the mentally ill, and people with epilepsy. Minnesota's law was primarily applied to white working-class women considered to be feebleminded (Ladd-Taylor, 2011, p. 118). Feeblemindedness was mostly diagnosed by means of an intelligence test. As Ladd-Taylor writes about a case from the year 1937: "After IQ tests found both parents to be feebleminded, they were committed to state guardianship, sent to the state institution and sterilized." (p. 117).

How about the scientific basis for such consequential decisions? Harry Sharp, main promoter of Indiana's compulsory sterilization law of 1907, said many years later: "We did not know enough about science then." (Carlson, 2011, p. 21).

First, it should have been clarified whether intelligence tests really were the appropriate means for diagnosing feeblemindedness, and, above all, whether there even is a sufficiently clear definition of feeblemindedness in the first place. As early as 1928 Goddard, a decided advocate of the concept of feeblemindedness, of its diagnose through intelligence tests, and of its high heritability, stated: "It was for a time rather carelessly assumed that everybody who tested 12 years or less was feebleminded ... We now know, of course, that only a small percentage of the people who test 12 are actually feeble-minded – that is, are incapable of managing their affairs with ordinary prudence or of competing in the struggle for existence." (Goddard, 1928, p. 220).

Furthermore, there should have been unambiguous evidence for intelligence in general, and for feeblemindedness in particular, as being heritable. As early as 1937, Lewis Terman, formerly a firm believer in the heritability of intelligence, expressed some doubt, "Nor should it be necessary to point out that such data do not, in themselves, offer any conclusive evidence of the relative contributions of genetic and environmental factors in determining the mean differences observed." (Terman & Merrill, 1937). The phrasings "We now know, of course" (Goddard) and "Nor should it be necessary to point out" (Terman) are, by the way, quite interesting. Both had not long before firmly asserted the opposite of what they now find self-evident and as not needing to be pointed out.

Goddard and Terman are both extreme examples of an overestimation of the significance of the heritability of intelligence as well as of the predictive power of intelligence tests. In the end they were scientists enough to be led to a revision of their opinion on the strength of the data. We will see that in the field of research we are dealing with here this is rather the exception than the rule. Furthermore they did not try to intentionally provoke an impression about the heritability of intelligence not born out by the data, something which in this field of research is no matter of course either.

Immigration and the intelligence of the nation

If we widen the meaning of the term "eugenics" a little, we may consider immigration laws to be eugenic measures, too, in so far as they intend to protect the genetic state of the nation.[17] In the year 1924, the American Congress changed immigration quotas in disfavour of South and Southeast European countries on the basis of intelligence test data that had been collected in a huge intelligence testing project with First World War draftees and were thought to show an inferior intelligence of the people from those countries (Laughlin, 1924).[18] The psychologists who, via the official eugenics expert of the congressional committee, pleaded for a change in immigration quotas knew as little scientifically what they were doing as did the proponents of compulsory sterilization. Not only was the heritability of intelligence an unvalidated preconception, but in order to assess the eugenic effects of immigration with at least some degree of precision, the *degree* of heritability would have had to be known as well. Yet at that time the procedures for determining that degree, quantitative genetics, did not even exist yet. This shows the degree of carelessness with which the scientists approached such extremely consequential issues like immigration restrictions. Unfortunately we must fear, however, considering the scientifically unvalidated ideas prevailing among scientists about heritability and malleability of in-

---

17 In principle, the intent could also be to improve the genetic state, yet laws proposed or passed all had the above intent.
18 In order to refute the false assertion by Herrnstein and Murray (1994, see below) that intelligence test data had played no role in the Congressional hearings, Hirsch (1997) gives the intelligence test data presented to the congressional committee in facsimile.

telligence to this day, that quantitative genetic data, had they existed, would probably still have been used at that time as evidence *for* the restriction of immigration from South and Southeastern Europe. That little has changed in the minds of scientists since, can be seen from the fact that 100 years after that Immigration Act psychologists still plead for immigration restrictions on eugenic grounds, as do, for example, Herrnstein & Murray (1994, p. 359).[19] Herrnstein and Murray's book has generated a vast (and necessary) debate about xenophobia and racism (see, for example, Fraser, 1995). It is conspicuous, however, how little the debate is about science, and nowhere do we find the scientific proof, which could well be given, that immigration restrictions on eugenic grounds make no sense whatsoever because (1) the heritability of mental traits is utterly population specific (see above), (2) the heritability of a trait tells nothing about whether the differences between populations are genetically caused (see below), and (3) the heritability of a trait tells nothing about its malleability (see above). A scientific clarification of the issue has been overdue for decades. It could, for example, have made the debate in Germany about Sarrazin's proposal to restrict immigration from Turkey (Sarrazin, 2010) more factual and a lot shorter. That this scientific clarification has not happened is only to a lesser degree due to the intricacy of the issue. Chiefly it has to do with the fact that a coherent scientific discussion about what quantitative genetic data can tell about mental traits in humans and, more importantly, what they can *not* tell, has not at all occurred, even though all the results brought forward in favour of a high heritability of intelligence stem from quantitative genetic studies. Specifically the relation between heritability and malleability, which is decisive for the theoretical and practical value of heritability coefficients, should have been clarified conclusively on the basis of the partitioning of the phenotypic variance and the definition of the heritability coefficient. Instead, the partitioning of the variance, if addressed at all in the discussion, has only been specified in order to explain the heritability coefficient. The partitioning of the phenotypic variance and the heritability coefficient are rather simple mathematically and therefore easy to understand, but their contextual implications are not. If these implications, which by necessity lead to the above expressed insight that heritability coefficients for mental traits make no scientific sense whatsoever, are not dealt with, the reader is left confronted with the published heritability estimates over the whole range of possible values and may think about the heritability of intelligence and its significance for the immigration from Turkey into Germany what he likes. Intuitively he will however mostly think, that intelligence is largely heritable, and that the Turks, to whom, as it appears, psychology has attested a lesser intelligence, should stay in Turkey.

---

19 Murray is a political scientist

11⁺ – A tragedy unnoticed

11⁺ (eleven plus) was an intelligence test which had to be taken by every eleven year old child in England and Wales from 1944 to the mid 1960s. The result decided whether a child was allowed to go to a so-called "grammar school" which prepared for university or not. The chance to go to university when coming from one of the other public schools, the so-called "secondary modern" was minimal. About 20 % of children went to a grammar school. The scientific rationale for this selection system had been supplied by the psychologist Cyril Burt. It critically rested on the assumption of a high heritability of intelligence.

Burt believed to have two reasons for his assumption of a high heritability of intelligence, one based on the g-factor and the other one on results of twin studies. The g-factor (g for general intelligence) is an invention by the British psychologist Charles Spearman, denoting a *general* capacity, present in different people to a different degree, to solve mental problems of the most diverse kinds. According to Spearman, intelligence can best be described by this general factor, while other researchers found it more reasonable to describe intelligence in the form of several *specific* factors, like verbal or mathematical intelligence. Spearman also developed the mathematical procedure for finding such factors (the g-factor or specific factors), "factor analysis". With no consensus about the structure of intelligence existing (neither as to the significance of g nor as to the number of specific factors necessary to describe intelligence) after more than 100 years of applying the procedure, we may assume that there is no (and will not be any) binding description of the structure of intelligence, as there can be no criteria for deciding what description of the structure of intelligence is to be seen as more sensible than another one.[20] Ultimately the debate suffers from the fact that there cannot possibly be a binding definition of intelligence. Whether to view athletic or musical achievements as factors of intelligence, for example, as has been proposed by Howard Gardner (e.g. 1983), is lastly up to one's personal whim. Depending on his interests, anyone can pick those mental capacities from the infinite number of possible ones which he deems worth to be considered as part of intelligence. All this demonstrates that factors of intelligence do not represent realities independent of the human mind, as do cells or planets, but products of the human mind, so-called "constructs" or "hypothetical constructs". Whatever role one may assign to the g-factor with respect to the structure of intelligence, the question is to be asked whether this factor, which results from the most diverse mental tasks correlating with each other (who does

---

20 In fields of application (e.g. vocational counselling), it must be decided in each single case as to what aspect of intelligence, whether a more general one or one or more specific ones, is relevant for a prediction of future behaviour.

well in one tends to do so in any other one), tells us anything about the heritability of intelligence, as Spearman and many intelligence researchers after him have assumed.

There are no empirical data about biological or social causes of the fact that all mental tasks correlate to some degree, so that we may only speculate about those causes. Concerning biological causes one might speculate, for example, that there are genetically caused differences in membrane characteristics of neurons to the effect that neuronal processes proceed at different speeds, which causes mental processes to proceed at different speeds, which then leads to differences in the capacity to solve all kinds of mental problems. But we may as well speculate that different social experiences (e.g. at school or within families) effect that people differ in their motivation to solve mental problems, or to generally excel intellectually, irrespective of the kind of the problems to be solved. And quite obviously there are huge differences between families, for example, as to the amount of emphasis laid on mental achievements, no matter what their kind. As a consequence there must be correlations between the most diverse mental tasks, meaning that a person who does well in one mental task tends to do so in any other, too.

The examples show that the g-factor may not in itself indicate intelligence to be heritable, as it may as well be determined by social as by biological conditions.[21]

The second reason for Burt's firm belief in a high heritability of intelligence was provided by the results of his twin studies.

When the British King in 1946 knighted the psychologist Cyril Burt on account of his great scientific achievements, he could not foresee what the psychologist Leon Kamin found out 25 years later: a large part of the data from Burt's twin studies were fabricated or manipulated (Kamin, 1974).[22] It has been argued (e.g. Jensen, 1995) that it is actually irrelevant whether Burt's data is acknowledged or not, because later studies confirmed his results. But even though there were indeed studies confirming his results, i.e. showing a high degree of heritability of intelligence, there were others that found much smaller heritability values or even no heritability at all (see p. 18). In addition, Burt's data played a particularly influential role in the contentious debate. Due to their author's prominence and the very large (alleged) sample sizes of Burt's studies they had a large scientific impact. The notion of a high heritability of intelligence has been enormously enhanced by Burt's dubious data.

---

21 As to the psychology of the common misconception of the g-factor automatically indicating heritability of intelligence, see more below in the context of Jensen's idea that the g-factor has been *discovered*.
22 Comments on the case can be found in Mackintosh (1995a).

After what has been said in the first part of this book about coefficients of heritability (that they may take on nearly any possible value and tell nothing about the malleability of intelligence), it is, scientifically speaking, actually rather inessential whether one pays attention to Burt's data or not. But this in no way means that it is inessential whether one pays attention to the Burt-scandal or not. The affair is quite revealing in terms of how use is made of data and facts in the scientific community in as far as it deals with the heritability of intelligence. Jensen (1995) finds that Burt is at times "careless and eccentric" in presenting his results (p. 11), and even Mackintosh, who actually is very critical of Burt's manipulations (he writes, for example, that "... he (Burt) at best is guilty of deliberately misleading his readers..." (Mackintosh 1955 b, p. 68)) finds that "...he had a relatively *cavalier* attitude to the reporting of empirical data." (Mackintosh, 1995c, p. 148, italics mine). After reading Brand's (1995) review of Mackintosh's book one may even have the impression that the whole affair was a mere trifle because, as Brand reflects, Kepler, Newton, and Freud had an inclination toward manipulating data, too. As to this kind of reevaluation of the Burt scandal, the psychologist Franz Samelson worriedly asked: "What have we learned, not about IQ heritability, but about our discipline, our standards of science, our ethical standards in action, from the handling of this embarrassing affair?" (Samelson, 1996, p. 1178) and implicitly answers it in a later article about the affair with an ill concealed "nothing at all" (Samelson, 1997).

As for the scientific basis of the above mentioned 11^+ test, the assumption of a high heritability of intelligence plays an important, if not the decisive part. Quite as if it were a logical consequence of high heritability, it was also assumed that intelligence was largely unchangeable. Only under these premises, it could be assumed that an intelligence test taken at the age of eleven would allow a good prediction of achievements accomplished many years later (e.g. at university). Burt saw the positive effect of indiscriminately testing all eleven-year olds in public schools in the insufficiently qualified being in that way saved from failing in higher education.

Before addressing the social and psychological impact of the 11^+ law, which was in effect for 20 years, let us shortly look back at what is to be thought of Burt's assumptions scientifically: (1) the g-factor does not tell anything about the heritability of intelligence, (2) the data from Burt's twin studies were largely fabricated, and (3) the heritability of intelligence says practically nothing about its malleability anyway. On this shaky basis decisions were made about the destiny of millions of children.

A simple graph (figure 2) may visualize the order of magnitude of the tragedy, which was nonetheless not recognized as such by most of society. On the horizontal we find the 11^+ test performance, on the vertical the performance in higher education. Most pupils we find within the ellipse, each one with a testing

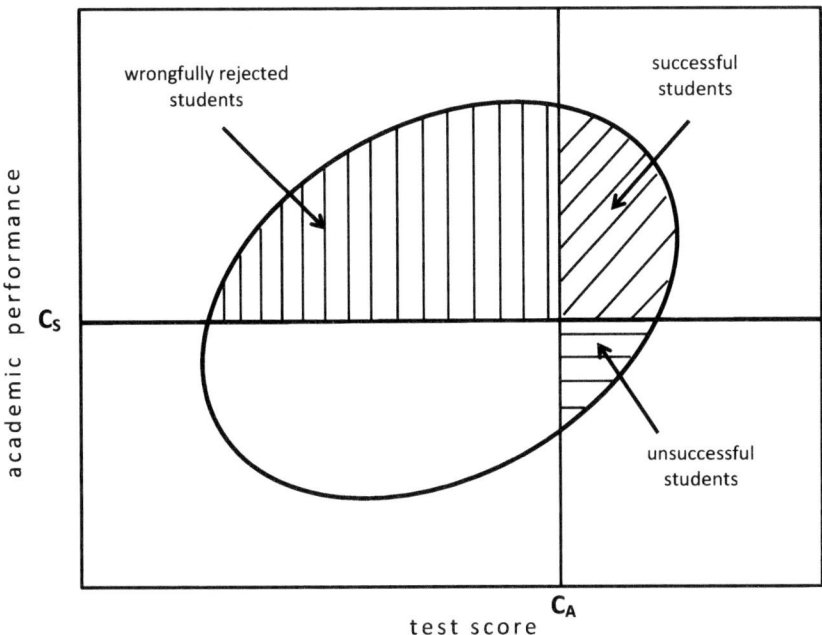

Figure 2. Relation between test intelligence and academic achievement, as well as the consequences of 11⁺.

score and a score for academic achievement.[23] (There are no values shown for single students). The distribution of the measurement pairs (one score for 11⁺ and one for academic achievement) represented by the ellipse, is typical for the correlation between intelligence test scores and performance in school or at university (see below). It may be mentioned that the density of measurement pairs (single points, as mentioned not shown in the graph) is at its maximum at the center of the ellipse and drops off in every direction away from that center. C_A on the test score axis is the critical value necessary for admission to a grammar school. C_S on the axis of academic performance is the critical value for success (degree received) at university. C_A is positioned in such a way that about 20 % of the eleven-year olds attain or surpass it, as was the case at the time in England and Wales. C_S is positioned in a way that the proportion of students dropping out or failing in the exams is rather small, as was (and is) the case with British universities (horizontally hatched area). The crucial area is the vertically hatched one, which represents the proportion of students, who de facto were denied access to university even though they would have been successful there.

---

23 For students not admitted to higher education the academic achievement scores are the ones they would have attained if admitted.

The graph is just meant to give an idea of the order of magnitude of the different proportions of students. The form of the ellipse as well as the positions of C_A and C_S might have been somewhat different, but the proportion of wrongfully rejected students was at an rate substantial. Taking the population of England and Wales and a period of 20 years into account, we are dealing with millions of individual fates.

The decisive cause for the huge order of magnitude of the tragedy (one might as well speak of a catastrophe) is the low correlation between test intelligence and success in school or at university. Interestingly, the correlation is not seen as low at all in the field of psychology. The above mentioned task force installed by the American Psychological Association in order to document the scientific state of affairs in intelligence research gives a correlation of about .5 for the relation between test intelligence and success in school (the correlation with achievement at university should be somewhat lower still) and writes that test intelligence predicts success in school "fairly well" (Neisser et al., 1996). The task force seems to have felt compelled, however, to point out that a correlation of .5 means that just 25 % of the variance in school performance is due to differences in intelligence between students, meaning that if all students had the same intelligence 75 % of the differences in school performance would still be there. This is actually in crass contrast to the affirmation that test intelligence predicts school performance "fairly well". With such a small association it would be reasonable not to speak of "prediction" in the first place. Psychology obviously has developed its own inveterate use of language here, such that even a variable that explains less than 1 % of the variance of some other one is termed a "predictor", as, for example, happens to be the case with the psychological "predictor" of coronary disease, the so-called "Type A behaviour pattern" (Booth-Kewley & Friedman, 1987).

Putting to shame the scientists it was in the end *politicians*, not scientists, who saw that the predictive power of 11$^+$ had been greatly exaggerated and in no way justified the grave consequences of its implementation by law. A quote betrays the attitude of the minister of education and science, Anthony Crossland, toward the 11$^+$ system: "… I'm going to destroy every f—ing grammar school in England." (Murdoch, 2007, p. 155). Accordingly the system was abolished in the largest part of the United Kingdom in the mid 1960s.

Scientific racism[24]

Scientific racism is closely connected to the notion that intelligence is heritable. Among Darwin's "intellectual and moral faculties," the intellectual ones in particular were those which were supposedly less well developed in the "savages", which mostly meant the blacks (e. g. Darwin, 2004/1879, p. 45), a prejudice quite common to this day. As soon as the belief had developed that intellectual faculties were measurable, first via cranial capacity, later by means of tests of intelligence, scientific work on racial differences has nearly exclusively focused on those faculties. The decisive role in the study of racial differences was played by the prevalent fallacy: "intelligence is heritable – there are obvious genetic differences between races – so the difference between races as to intelligence (the mean test scores for blacks are lower than the ones for whites) must have a genetic basis." This is the essence of the racist ideology: there are genetically caused differences between races with respect to intelligence and, closely connected to this, with respect to moral quality. Looking at the sheer mass of scientific literature (I hesitate to write the term scientific without quotation marks) about racial differences, one may come to the conclusion that this is no prejudice any more, but a scientifically proven fact. Yet looking somewhat more closely into the matter one soon discovers that it is a relatively small, yet highly active group of psychologists who work on the topic and regularly come to the conclusion "Blacks are the least intelligent" (see below).

At Darwin's time it was not seen as a prejudice to think of the "savages" (mostly meaning the blacks) as being less intelligent, and even Darwin, an excellent observer of differences and similarities between living things by profession, deemed them to be on an earlier stage of evolutionary development than Europeans. It should be mentioned, however, that this Victorian view was not inevitably held. Alfred Russel Wallace, for example, who had developed evolution theory independently from Darwin, saw no significant differences between the "savages" and the Europeans with regard to intellectual and moral faculties (Wallace, 1869). The reason is probably quite a simple one: in contrast to Darwin he had lived together with those savages for years.

At the latest since the civil rights movement in the last century,[25] scientists can

---

24 The term is actually a contradiction in itself because racism, an ideology, cannot be scientific. One should rather speak of racism in science. Yet the term has come into use. Tucker's (2002) book about the topic, for example, has the title "The Funding of Scientific Racism."
25 Two decisive years are 1955 (Rosa Parks refuses to yield her seat in the bus to a white person as required by law) and 1957 (President Eisenhower sends the National Guard to Little Rock, Arkansas, in order to escort nine black students into a school only frequented by whites till then. In order that the racists really understood that times had changed he sent the most famous unit of the Second World War, the 101st Airborne Division, right with it).

no more make openly racist statements. Racial differences must be scientifically substantiated since, according to the (quite correct) motto: "Science is about what is factually, not politically correct". The main emphasis in the study of racial differences with respect to psychological traits has been on differences in intelligence. Notable figures in this expectably extremely controversial debate are the Canadian psychologist Philippe Rushton, the American psychologist Arthur Jensen, and the British psychologist Hans Jürgen Eysenck.

To call scientists who study racial differences racists makes little sense because it is impossible to know whether someone misuses science in order to promote racial prejudices or whether he actually believes in what he says or writes. Rushton may be seen as an exception, however. He has been the president of the "Pioneer Fund" which, as documented by Tucker (2002), has repeatedly financed racist projects. His attitude toward empirical evidence is characterized, for example, by his referring to "the ethnographic record" as a source of data, which turns out to be data published in 1898 (a time when scientific racism was common) by a French surgeon, whose name he does not reveal (Rushton, 1988, p. 1015).

His "theory" (in this case I *must* put quotation marks) about racial differences is of the evolutionary psychological kind, meaning that it claims to be based on evolution theory. According to it, blacks follow a "reproduction strategy" characterized by having many offspring and caring little about them. For that it takes high fertility yet little intelligence, which is why blacks have large genitalia and small brains. Ulric Neisser comments on the theory by saying that it turns his stomach (Neisser, 2004, p. 6).[26]

Arthur Jensen became known through a 124 page article in the *Harvard Educational Review* (Jensen, 1969) which prompted a controversy about racial differences and the heritability of intelligence still going on today. The controversy is largely ideological in nature (on both sides) and rarely deals with science. Jensen's article in itself pretty well characterizes the scientific level of the debate which is not about data but about their *interpretation*. The decisive data in Jensen's article show (1) a high heritability of intelligence, (2) a significant difference between blacks and whites with respect to intelligence, and (3) the relative lack of success of training programs for disadvantaged minorities which primarily consisted of blacks. Jensen's interpretations of the data were all wrong. He viewed the heritability of intelligence which had resulted from twin studies (see above) as a biological constant and did not see its population specificity

---

26 An extensive critique of the theory can be found in Zuckerman & Brody (1988). Unfortunately wild Darwinizing speculations have become so common in evolutionary psychology that serious scientists must spend time and effort on commenting on them, however nonsensical they may be.

(due to different amounts of environmental variation); he thought that the difference between blacks and whites in intelligence was genetic in origin due to the heritability of intelligence; and he thought that the relative lack of success of the training programs was caused by the high heritability of intelligence.[27] The fact that the heritability is not a biological constant and has practically nothing to do with its malleability results from what has been explained in the first part of this book. Heritability of a trait not saying anything about the cause of differences between groups with respect to that trait follows from simple logic because irrespective of the heritability within groups there always may be environmental differences between groups that cause a difference between them with respect to the trait. In the extreme it may even be possible that, given a 100 % heritability of a trait, a difference between groups may be 100 % environmentally caused. A simple example from the field of plant growth may elucidate this. Let us imagine that from an amount of seed two random samples are taken. One is planted in soil with a good plant growth solution, the other one on soil with the same solution except that the nitrogen is left out of it. In this case the difference in height between the plants within the samples is exclusively genetically caused (100 % heritability) as all those plants grow under the same conditions, while the difference between the samples (the plants of the second one are smaller) are exclusively caused by the environment (Lewontin, 1995, p.133).

It is actually trivial to point out that for interpreting data in an empirical science it is essential to know what the numbers stand for. But, dealing with the heritability of intelligence, this point is by no means trivial. Heritability coefficients are no biological constants and tell nothing about malleability, and, just because there are other (obvious) differences between races that *are* genetically caused, differences in intelligence between races need not be caused genetically. A particularly instructive example about the importance of the *meaning* of data (what they stand for) is given by Jensen with his "ecological" correlation between cranial capacity (corresponds to brain size) and IQ (Jensen, 1998, p. 442). He and a small group of scientists, who for decades have been asserting the intellectual inferiority of blacks, believe to have found differences in cranial capacity between races. To conclude from that that the lesser test intelligence of blacks is genetic in origin, there must be a correlation between cranial capacity and test intelligence. At first Jensen (on p. 147) gives a correlation of .4.[28] Later (p. 442) we find an astounding correlation of .998, the very

---

[27] The programs were, as the above mentioned task force found out, partly quite successful (Neisser et al., 1996).
[28] The same value is given by Rushton. Other scientists, like, for example, the paleontologist Pat Shipman (1994) do not see any relation (p. 198). In addition it has clearly been shown that brain size depends on mental training (e. g. Myers, 2004. p. 430; Barnett & Williams, 2004, p.

correlation he calls "ecological". To arrive at it, he had correlated the *means* for cranial capacity and the *medians* for intelligence of the three populations "mongoloids" (Asians), "caucasoids" (whites), and "negroids" (blacks) (Figure 3).

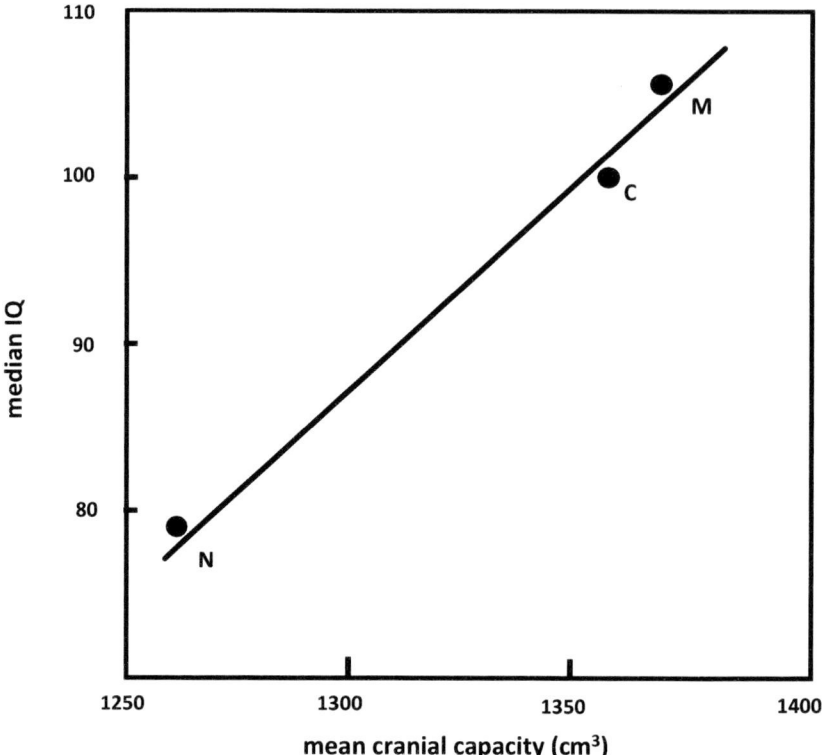

Figure 3. Relation between mean cranial capacity and median of IQ for blacks (N), whites (C) and Asians (M). (Jensen, 1998).

Irrespective of the validity of the data, this procedure implies that the three data points need only lie somehow along a straight line and a correlation close to unity must result because the individual differences have vanished due to the averaging and the forming of the medians. The way Jensen presents the "ecological" correlation, the reader is obviously supposed to believe that this is the actual, the *real* correlation. This ecological correlation (for whatever reason it is called that) is of course a huge overestimation of the correlation at issue here,

---

394; Kosslyn & Rosenberg, 2001, p. 285) which invalidates the whole causal interpretation (differences in intelligence between races as a consequence of differences in brain size).

and it is to be asked why Jensen presents this "ecological" correlation at all, as it is rather misleading in this context.[29]

Grave as such oddities may be, they pale against Jensen's proving himself to be without any awareness of a fundamental problem in the philosophy of science, one that is of consequence for psychology as for no other field of science. We find the proof in his 650 page strong book "The g Factor" even before the text has started. On a separate page he dedicates the book to Charles Spearman with the words

> Dedicated to the memory of
> CHARLES EDWARD SPEARMAN
> The discoverer of g

Spearman, who, with his name written in capital letters and with both forenames written in full here, stands before us in monumental greatness, had proposed the g factor based on a procedure he had developed, factor analysis, as the most important aspect of the structure of intelligence (see p. 34). So the g factor, a pure abstraction, has been invented (construed) and not discovered by Spearman. The distinction is not an epistemological subtlety but of fundamental importance and may, in case of being confused, have grave consequences. If we speak of a construct like intelligence or an intelligence factor found through factor analysis as having been *discovered*, we attribute an existence to it that is independent of the human mind the way microbes, islands, or species are. This misleading mental step is termed "reification". To take that step is tempting because we can envision something real and concrete more easily than something abstract and conceptual. In case of the g factor it is particularly tempting, as Spearman's invention may only be comprehended through the knowledge of the diverse procedural steps taken to derive it (development of subtests, application of these to a large sample of individuals, application of factor analysis to the resulting data). So it is a lot easier to think of the g factor as a factual entity residing in the brain. This is additionally helped by seeing the g factor as heritable, on account of genes coding for proteins which in turn participate in the forming of quite concrete bodily characteristics (e.g. in the form of brain structures). The reification of the highly abstract concept of intelligence into a bodily characteristic has probably been the main reason why its heritability has

---

29 Oddities in dealing with data and methods, as we find them on many occasions with Jensen, are not uncommon in the field of research about the heritability of intelligence, however, as the geneticist Richard Lewontin noted as early as 1975. In connection with the Eysenck case (p. 44–51), we will learn about some even more telling examples.

always implicitly been assumed even long before quantitative genetic studies seemed to confirm it.

As to differences between races, the flawed cognitive scheme applies: there are obvious genetically determined bodily differences between races, so a difference in intelligence must be genetic, too, especially if intelligence is "measured" through cranial capacity.

But let us keep in mind: only a small group of scientists, especially Philippe Rushton, Arthur Jensen, Richard Lynn, and Hans Jürgen Eysenck, all of them financially assisted by the Pioneer Fund, find race differences with respect to cranial capacity and a correlation between cranial capacity and test intelligence of up to .998.[30]

The Eysenck case

Near the end of this sinister chapter, let us turn to the psychologist Hans Jürgen Eysenck who, like nobody else, has shown us what we may encounter, as to the use of data and methods, when we take a closer look at the scientific literature about the topic of "heritability of intelligence".

Besides John Watson and Burrhus Skinner, Hans Jürgen Eysenck has probably left the strongest mark on psychology and its image in a broader public.[31] The blurb of his last book (Eysenck, 1998) mentions more than 1000 articles and more than 70 books in which Eysenck has made his ideas public, popular books among them of which large numbers of copies have been sold. Eysenck's central themes over more than half a century were (1) the propagation of psychology as a natural science, (2) intelligence research (the heritability of intelligence in particular)[32], and (3) genetically caused differences between races with respect to intelligence. In accordance with his particular esteem for intelligence as a personality dimension, the title of his last book is "Intelligence" (Eysenck, 1998). In it he once again explicitly discusses race differences. As for psychology as a natural science, a postulate promulgated by John Watson (1913), probably no psychologist has been more successful in spreading the idea among scientists

---

[30] Of course Rushton and his comrades-in-arms do not see themselves as racists, and it actually makes no sense to name them so because it will never be possible to determine with certainty whether their motivation is a scientific or a racist one. Occasionally they even succeeded in posturing as brave defenders of the freedom of science and as fighters against ideologically based demands of "political correctness". That they are not has been shown by Tucker (2002) who documented their close connection to the intellectual right wing scene.

[31] This applies to so-called "academic" psychology. Freud, clearly the most famous of all psychologists, and his psychoanalysis play a part of their own in the history of psychology..

[32] For other mental traits, like, for example, one of his personality dimensions, neuroticism, he also postulated a biological and heritable basis

and in a wider public than Eysenck. On that account he is very eager to demonstrate that he, too, has a firm grasp of the exact and technological sciences, like, for example, quantum physics (Eysenck, 1998, p. 5) or cosmology (p. 8). When posturing like that, blunders are rather inevitable, like when he deems the turbocharger to be a kind of fuel injection (p. 75).[33] Well, no student of engineering will read Eysenck's musings and be irritated by them. Yet, as to the heritability of intelligence and genetically caused differences in intelligence between races, quite a few students will read the deliberations of one of the most famous psychologists who is known to have dealt with just that topic for a long time and in great detail. Together with Jensen, Eysenck has for decades been at the center of the controversy about the heritability of intelligence and about the alleged genetic basis of race differences with respect to intelligence. For him there was an "overwhelming importance of genetic factors producing the great variety of intellectual differences ... and much of the differences observed between certain racial groups." (Eysenck, 1971, p. 130).[34] Considering the extreme social explosiveness inherent in the topic, we may assume that Eysenck had a particularly firm grasp of the scientific fundamentals of the discussion. The mere thought that this might not be so would probably have been considered an outrage by the famous psychologist, and with Eysenck being that famous and with him so much stressing his natural scientific competence, nobody has dared to voice that thought. But the field "heritability of intelligence" is full of surprises and someone who has dealt a little more closely with Eysenck's deliberations knows that Eysenck is too.[35] Let us therefore simply have a closer look at what Eysenck has to say about the fundamental methodological concepts of heritability estimates. Two of the most important ones of those concepts are the ones of "regression" and of "interaction".

As we have seen, the regression effect was first described by Galton (p. 27). Because he had observed it with parent/child correlations and because he, at the time, was preoccupied with inheritance, he deemed the regression effect to be a biological law. With the emergence of correlation and regression statistics, it soon became clear, however, that the effect occurs generally with correlations between any kind of variables and has essentially nothing to do with biology.

Regardless of what correlation and regression statistics may say, more than 100 years after Galton, Eysenck (1998) still finds the regression effect to be a biological law, expressly emphasizing the term "biological" (p. 39). In contrast to Galton, who at his time could not have known anything about genetics in today's

---

33 The turbocharger delivers air, not fuel, into the combustion chamber
34 Only in his last book did he modify his claim of a genetically caused difference in intelligence between blacks and whites a little.
35 He held, for example, that lung cancer has nothing to do with smoking (e. g. Eysenck, 1987).

sense, Eysenck believed to have found the basis of this biological law, namely in deliberations by Li (1971) about the effects of chance segregation and recombination of genes in meiotic cell division. However he evidently has not grasped their statistical implications as he asserts, with an explicit reference to Li, that these chance processes cause the regression effect and the regression effect must thus be a biological law (Eysenck, 1973, p. 132). Those chance processes do of course contribute to the regression effect because they codetermine the parent/offspring correlation, but they do not determine the correlation exclusively, because, as with all biological and psychological variables one may think of, and mental traits in particular, the environment plays a part (at times, as we have seen, by far the more significant one) and codetermines parent/child correlation and regression. But regression may not be seen as a biological law for the simple reason alone that it occurs with *any* correlation between variables and not only with the correlations that reflect the resemblance of relatives as they are used in quantitative genetics.[36]

A misunderstanding cannot be more fundamental and have graver consequences than Eysenck's ideas about regression. Even if we for once consider regression exclusively in the context of the resemblance between parents and their children (or any other relatives), the notion of regression as a biological law automatically leads to ignoring the role of the environment. The resemblance between parents and their children is caused by common genes (50 %) and a partly common environment. Both together determine the size of the regression effect. So seeing it as a biological law automatically means interpreting the whole resemblance between parents and their children as genetically caused. Consequently (and nonsensically) Eysenck presents a formula, allegedly developed by geneticists, for predicting the IQ of a child from the mean IQ of its parents (Eysenck, 1973, p. 105):

$$O = M + h_N^2(P - M)$$

where O is the IQ predicted, P the mean IQ of the parents, M the population mean and h_N^2 the heritability coefficient.[37] But why use the *heritability coefficient* which

---

36 For determining the resemblance of relatives, the *same* variable (e. g. body size) is measured in different groups of relatives (e.g. parents and their children). Most correlations in psychology are ones between *different* variables measured in the same individuals, like, for example, the performance in two (or more) different tasks as we have seen in connection with the structure of intelligence (p. 34). Rather needless to say that there may be correlations (and regression effects) between variables that are neither biological nor psychological, like, for example, atmospheric pressure and time of sunshine.

37 In order to facilitate the understanding of the formula for a reader probably accustomed to

of course reflects the genetic effect alone, for the prediction? The resemblance between parents and their children with respect to intelligence does not only depend on them partly sharing their genes, but also on them partly sharing the environment. So the question emerges why Eysenck does not use the common regression equation for his prediction as anyone familiar with correlation and regression statistics would do:

$$O = M_C + b_{PC}(P - M_P)$$

where O stands for the IQ predicted, M_C for the mean for all children, P for the mean of the two parents, M_P for the mean of all parents and b_{PC} for the parent/child regression coefficient which is determined by the genetic *plus* the environmental similarity of parents and their children and thus naturally allows a better prediction?[38] There are only two possible answers to this question: either Eysenck does not know that for predictions with quantitative variables a formal tool has been developed, correlation and regression statistics,[39] or he believes that the regression and the heritability coefficients are identical. The former one would have to assume if h_N^2 in his formula indeed symbolized the heritability coefficient (which is what he writes). If he were familiar with regression statistics he would have to know that the regression coefficient, which incorporates the effect of the environment, allows for a better prediction. The latter alternative is suggested by his own wording, like when he writes, "We can determine the heritability of intelligence by looking at the amount of regression." (Eysenck, 1998, p. 39), as well as by his largely inflated heritability values, which may actually be regression values. As if he wanted to further prove his ignorance concerning quantitative genetics he writes in the same context: "If heritability is 100 % there is no regression." (p. 39). But with parents and their children only having 50 % of their genes in common, there would only be a correlation (and no functional relation) between the IQ of parents and children even with 100 % heritability and therefore a regression effect, too.[40]

Unbelievable as all this may appear with such a famous psychologist allegedly committed to natural scientific rigor, things do not look better for Eysenck's

---

having the variables in an equation represented by x and y, let it be noted that the variables are O (for y) and P (for x), while M and h_N^2 are empirically derived constants.

38 Let us ignore the minor mistake in Eysenck's equation of him using the population mean instead of the means of the children and parents, respectively.

39 It is mostly applied to the relation between different variables, but may also be applied to the same variable if measured in different groups, like parents and children (see note 36, p. 46).

40 Even if parents and children did have 100 % of their genes in common, there would, the environments of parents and children not being identical, still only be a correlation (and no functional relation) and thus still a regression effect. Again we see that Eysenck totally ignores environmental effects.

competence with respect to a further concept of extreme significance for quantitative genetics, interaction.

The great significance of interaction effects for quantitative genetics simply follows from the fact that part of the phenotypic variance can be caused by such effects (see, for example, formula (3), p. 11). As outlined above they come about if under specific conditional constellations (e. g. if a specific genetic constellation coincides with a specific environmental one) the effects that both conditions on average have on the variable measured (e. g. intelligence) do not simply add up but result in a value larger or smaller than the sum of those two average effects. So it may happen, for example, that a specific environmental condition does not always have the same effect, no matter what genetic constellation it is combined with, but that the effect differs according to the genetic constellation it is combined with.

In order to graphically illustrate the interaction effect, the result of an experiment in which two genetically different strains of rats were raised under three different environmental conditions is often depicted by way of an example (Cooper & Zubek, 1958). The behavioural variable on which the effect of the two genetic and the three environmental conditions was tested was the number of errors the animals made in a maze. Two strains of rats had been bred which were clearly different with respect to the average number of errors they made in the maze: "dull" rats (many errors) and "bright" rats (fewer errors) so to speak. For each strain three groups were formed, each raised under a different environmental condition, an "impoverished" condition (the animals were raised alone), a "normal" condition (they were raised together with other animals), and an "enriched" environment (they were raised together with other animals and diverse objects they could play with). Figure 4 shows the results.

One can see that the strains only differed substantially under the normal environmental condition, i. e. the one they were bred to be either dull or bright under. Under the enriched environment, the dull rats just made a few more errors than the bright ones, and under the impoverished condition, the number of errors is even identical for the two strains. For this condition, the interaction effect can be discerned quite clearly. Compared to the normal condition it means a disproportionate rise in the number of errors for the bright rats. For the condition "enriched" the interaction can be seen in the form of a disproportionate decline in the number of errors for the dull rats.[41] Obviously the effect of the genetic difference between the two strains is not the same under all environmental conditions but depends on the specific environmental condition. Under the normal condition it is large, under the enriched one small and under

---

41 The amount of interaction can be seen by the degree to which the dotted and the solid lines are not parallel.

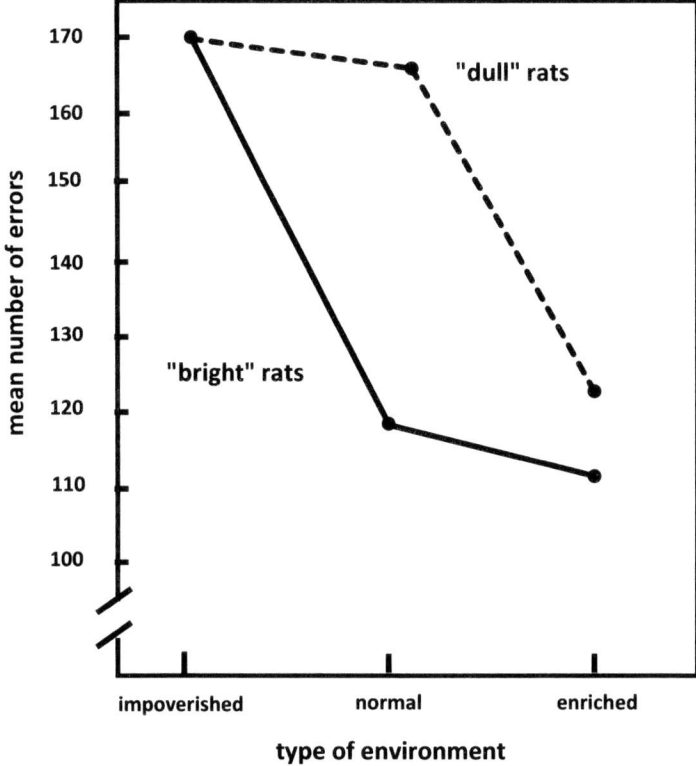

Figure 4. Mean number of errors made in a maze for two genetically different strains of rats raised under three different conditions (Cooper & Zubek, 1958).

the impoverished one there is no difference whatsoever in the number of errors between the two genetically different groups. It is easy to imagine that with regard to the development of intelligence in humans there may be large interaction effects, too.

Eysenck (1998) occasionally uses the term "interaction" in the chapter about genetic and environmental aspects of intelligence, yet gives no definition. One might assume that he takes familiarity of the concept of interaction for granted, yet it can nowhere be seen that with the term as he uses it he actually means interaction in the statistical sense, which alone is relevant in this context. Quite to the contrary, in his formula about the partitioning of phenotypic variance (he erroneously speaks of the fundamental formula of *behavioural* genetics instead of *quantitative* genetics), the proportion due to interaction is missing entirely, quite like already 25 years earlier (Eysenck, 1973, p. 88). One might think that this omission was made to just simplify things. Earlier he writes, however, that genes and environment are interactive forces, which indicates that he deems interaction to be a simple addition of effects. In the same vein we read several pages later (Eysenck, 1998, p. 43) that the phenotype of an individual comes about by the interaction of genotype and environment. Here, too, we cannot be dealing with interaction in the statistical sense, because interaction in the statistical sense is not the only thing that determines the phenotype. One page later we encounter the term "interaction" again, this time in the context of the experiment by Cooper and Zubek (figure 4), where, as described, a conspicuous interaction can be seen. It can however not be assumed that Eysenck has recognized the interaction effect in this example, though it was given by himself. For had he recognized it, it should have absolutely compelled him to include the part of variance due to interaction in his fundamental formula.[42] After all, the most interesting thing in that experiment is precisely the gene/environment interaction, which is why it is referred to so frequently.

In whatever way we read Eysenck's texts about gene/environment interaction, it is difficult to escape the impression that he simply does not know what interaction is and that he sees any effects that result from combinations of conditions (e.g. a specific genetic one combined with a specific environmental one) as interaction effects, be they additive or interactive. Considering his ideas about the concept of regression, this need not surprise us all too much anymore.

As mentioned, the second part of this book is supposed to bring home to the reader that research about the heritability of intelligence often follows its own rules and that these, if we can at all consider them as something close to rules, are not necessarily the ones we otherwise know from science, like the simple rule, for example, that a scientist must be familiar with the terms he uses. Eysenck may in this respect be an extreme example. Beyond this, however, a short additional comment seems appropriate in this case, because Eysenck has been influential among such a wide public.

Intelligence, its heritability and the causes of differences between races, has been a central topic for Eysenck throughout his whole scientific life. In particular, he has most provocatively maintained in this context that differences between races have a genetic basis and that the high heritability of intelligence implies that intervention measures for disadvantaged minorities make little sense. Assertions of such social and political explosiveness he was only able to proclaim by referring to alleged scientific facts. To do this, he of course had to posture as a renowned scientific expert. This expert on questions about the heritability of mental traits then confuses the regression and the heritability coefficients, deems the statistical regression effect to be a biological law, finds

---

[42] It would of course be appropriate, particularly with respect to the missing experimental control with heritability estimates in humans, to also mention the variation due to gene/environment *covariation*.

that statistical interaction is the summation of effects, finds that, when making inferences from the parents' intelligence to that of their children, the common environment of parents and children plays no role, and believes that in the case of a 100 % heritability of a trait there is no parent/child regression effect.

How is something positively unbelievable like this possible?

Whatever the reasons may be in detail, one thing is obvious: In this field of research as it has established itself, the correctives are missing which could prevent something like this from happening. In any science, errors and nonsense may remain undetected for a while. But if they remain unrectified, though propagated over decades by one of its most prominent members, the question must be asked about the scientific standards of the field, as Samelson did after the Burt scandal (see p. 36).

In the often bitterly contested debate about racial differences, it has been seen as a scandal by many that psychologists propagate views which further racist thinking and have their studies financed by a racist institution (the Pioneer Fund) and their views published in right wing organs (e.g. the Mankind Quarterly). But from a scientific perspective, the scandal must rather be seen in the fact that the scientific community has been unable to prevent racist ideas from being spread, veiled as science due to the lack of scientific rigor in the field.[43]

Molecular genetic peculiarities

Philip Kitcher's dictum "Life has not been kind to human behavioral geneticists" (Kitcher, 1996, p. 254) is still unreservedly valid today. Momentarily it is mainly the *molecular* human behavioural geneticists that life demands much of.

The first to raise hopes of advancing to the molecular basis of a particular behavior (homosexuality) was the geneticist Dean Hamer (e.g. Hamer & Copeland, 1994). But when the gene for homosexuality stubbornly evaded its identification he came up with some other gene, this time quite a concrete one (VMAT2), the "GODgene" (Hamer, 2004), which he supposed to prompt spirituality and self transcendence in its carrier if present in the right form. More interesting than the gene itself (it has nothing to do with belief in God) is the kind

---

[43] So Neisser, for example (see p. 40) could not simply write about Rushton's "theory" of racial differences what in a serious science anyone would immediately recognize, namely that it consists of groundless and unvalidatable speculations, but could only resort to the non-scientific comment that it turned his stomach.

of its promotion to GODgene. Belief in God being an emotional rather than a rational matter, one simply turn to the bodily substances known to be closely related to emotional processes and soon one will come across the monoamines like serotonin or dopamine. Of a gene participating in the production of these substances one then find two forms the carriers of which differ minimally as to their scores on a spirituality questionnaire: voilà, the GODgene! All we know about the gene, provided the result will be replicated in the first place, is that via an unknown emotional process, it has a minimal effect on the scores attained on a spirituality scale.

The scientific recognition has so far been denied to the GODgene (and will arguably stay denied) but outside the science community life has finally been quite kind to Hamer, as his book managed to occupy the front page of TIME International (29th of November, 2004) and will thus probably have made its author rich.

As mentioned, the gene for homosexuality continues to evade its identification. But it still stays on the agenda despite no new empirical evidence for it. How something like that is accomplished has been demonstrated by Savolainen and Lehmann (2007). They presumed that there is one single gene for homosexuality (which is extremely improbable) and performed diverse population genetic computations which showed that under specific evolutionary conditions this gene could be advantageous with respect to selection. Nobody knows (and can possibly know) whether these conditions ever existed during evolution but the study at least makes sure that the genetic basis of homosexuality will continue to stay an issue.

As to intelligence, we have seen in the first part of this book (p. 23) that there are no molecular genetic indications whatsoever for intelligence to be heritable to more than a minimal degree. As mentioned, however, the procedures for its determination are still in a kind of testing phase. Amazingly the above mentioned procedures of SNP analysis (p. 22), when applied to the variable "creativity", yielded a value of 9 % phenotypic variance explained by genetic differences (Reuter, 2006), a value beefed up by Reuter a year later to 14 % (Reuter, 2007). The results have not been replicated and it must be asked how such values could have come about when the values for intelligence, the psychological variable for which the highest heritability has been assumed by many, are all below 1 % and the one for body size, a variable definitely heritable to a high degree, is just around 5 %.

The complete absence of valid, i. e. replicated, molecular genetic evidence for the heritability of mental traits has in no way motivated the researchers in the field, however, to act with somewhat more reservation when propagating that heritability. Quite to the contrary they have presented alleged indirect molecular genetic evidence (evidence not based on SNP analysis) for a genetic basis of mental traits, which is obviously supposed to evoke the impression that there can be no doubts about a close connection between the DNA and mental traits. After what we have so far encountered in the field, we must take a closer look at that evidence.

It is most prominently Robert Plomin who not only, like many others, has declared a high heritability of intelligence on the basis of quantitative genetic studies, but who has also for many years predicted the molecular genetic proof for it. Even before he could try to provide this proof due to the technological progress in analysing the DNA, he claimed to have demonstrated a molecular genetic basis of mental traits (Plomin et al., 1990). His use of language alone is supposed to make that basis quite clear: "Behavior is a phenotype – that is, an observable characteristic we can measure" (p. 2). The custom to call every behaviour and every trait a "phenotype" is quite common among psychological behavioral geneticists. In genetics, however, a "phenotype" makes only sense in connection with a "genotype", which Plomin mentions no sooner than 30 pages later. The genotype is the genetic constellation that participates (together with the environment) in the creation of the phenotype. If there is no genetic basis of a trait one does not speak of a phenotype. To generally call all kinds of behaviour "phenotypes" insinuates that there is a genetic basis for all of them.

According to Plomin one concrete example for the genetic basis of a mental trait is albinism (p. 53–55), a genetically caused disorder characterized by a deficit or the complete absence of pigment in the skin, hair and iris, or the iris alone. Plomin draws the connection to psychology by claiming that albinism implies an increased emotionality, such that albinism is supposed to be a "pleiotropy", i.e. an effect of a mutation on two or more traits. The alleged increased emotionality was evidenced in mice by means of the so-called "open field-test". For this purpose the animals are put into a brightly lit enclosure, an environment obviously straining for them. The behaviour recorded in order to measure emotionality is defecation and urination (correlated positively with emotionality) and the degree of exploration behaviour (correlated negatively with emotionality). Mice with albinism show a higher emotionality in the open field than mice without the mutation. The authors assume that the effect is "mediated by the visual system". After having found out that the difference in emotional behaviour between the albino mice and mice with pigment was smaller under red light, the authors developed the hypothesis that albino mice are afraid of the light in the open field, that they may be "photophobic". The phrasing that the effect may be "mediated by the visual system" and that the authors developed the "hypothesis that the albino mice were afraid of the light in the open field" is quite interesting if compared with the phrasing one would normally use, which would be something like, "There is a reduced amount of pigment in the iris of the albino mice, which means that much more light falls onto their retinae, the light sensitive parts of the eye. As a consequence, they are photophobic, a symptom the authors need not assume hypothetically because it is listed in medical textbooks for all kinds of albinism" (e.g. Brenton, 1996).[44] Now why this odd phrasing in Plomin et al.? Simply because a normal phrasing would immediately reveal the nonsensical nature of the alleged pleiotropy. The albino mice are not more emotional, they are just photophobic and they are so for the most simple and unpsychological of all reasons: with the same illumination more light falls into their eyes than into those of the pigmented mice.

The whole thing has absolutely nothing to do with behavioural genetics. According to the authors' logic, hemophilia (a genetic disorder where blood coagulation is impaired) would constitute a pleiotropy, too, because people with the mutation carefully avoid being injured. So they have an injury phobia where the mutated gene would be the "injury avoidance gene".

In many places in the above mentioned book, as well as in its 6th edition, we find a reference to phenylketonuria as a behavioural genetic symptomatology. In this disease, if untreated, a mutation leads to a severe damage of the brain and, consequently, to mental retardation. But why phenylketonuria in a book about *behavioral* genetics? To be sure it is a genetic disease and this disease also affects behavior. But every severe genetic disease has an effect on behavior if only due to the psychological effects of suffering. The repeated mentioning of phenylketonuria in connection with intelligence establishes a purely associative and not a logical connection between the DNA and intelligence and thus somehow insinuates a genetic basis of intelligence. But how can phenylketonuria be a manifestation of the heritability of intelligence in a population in which the mutation does not occur in the first place?[45] There is neither a gene for mental retardation in phenylketonuria nor one for emotionality in albinism. In phenylketonuria there is just a genetic basis for a toxic accumulation of phenylalanine and its metabolites in the nervous system; and in albinism there is merely one for the lack of pigment in the iris. Mental retardation and emotionality are just side effects of a purely medical condition. The mentioning of the two diseases in a book about behavioural genetics obviously serves a single purpose: to evoke the impression that there is a molecular genetic basis for behavior and psychological traits.

Plomin's manner of evoking impressions like that can be particularly well observed in a comment he wrote about an article published in the journal *nature* in order to bring the molecular genetic basis of intelligence home to us. In that

---

44 Humans with the mutation tend to wear dark glasses.
45 A study about the heritability of intelligence should not include people with phenylketonuria because the genetic basis of intelligence sought after in such a study is not the one that causes phenylketonuria.

article (Deary et al., 2012) the authors show that 24 % of the variance of *change* of cognitive ability (intelligence) from childhood (11 years) to old age (65, 70 and 79 years) can be explained by genetic differences, measured in the form of SNP sequences (see p. 22). In the same issue of *nature* the article is commented on by Plomin. He starts with a quote from Galton: "There is no escape from the conclusion that nature prevails enormously over nurture." He reminds us of the contentious nature-nurture debate and then refers to the Deary et al. article with the remark that it "may mark the beginning of the end of the debate" because in it molecular genetic rather than quantitative genetic data are presented. Knowing Plomin as one of the firmest believers in a high heritability of intelligence, we now expect the debate to be decided in Galton's favor and Plomin indeed tries to present things quite that way. After shortly presenting the results of the Deary et al. study, he goes back to the heritability of intelligence issue with phrases like "The Deary et al. study may provide crucial clues for solving the missing heritability problem"[46] or that the study "... cannot quite mark the end of the nature-nurture controversy, it might be the beginning of the end." So we are now supposed to have the impression that the controversy about the heritability of intelligence will shortly be decided in favour of Galton (and Plomin). But the Deary et al. study does not tell anything about the heritability of intelligence at all. As mentioned it deals with factors that determine the *change* in intelligence over the life span (from 11 to 65, 70 or 79 years). As to the causes of the changes occurring over such a long time we should rather think of age-related degenerational processes of which it has been known for a long time that they are partly genetic in nature. So the genetic differences that account for 24 % of the variance in the change in intelligence over the life span are just the ones that account for the differences in the neurodegenerational processes of which the differences in the change in intelligence are a consequence, which means that they do not have anything to do with the heritability of intelligence.

The latest variant in the charade about the heritability of intelligence has been presented by Andy Coghlan (2012). Researchers at the University of California, Los Angeles, have found a gene, a mutation of which leads to a decrease in brain weight and as a consequence to a decrease in intelligence by 1.25 points. Quite like with phenylketonuria, the reduction in intelligence is the consequence of a pathological condition (in this case a rather mild one) and the gene in no way contributes to our knowledge about the heritability of intelligence because that heritability applies to people without the mutation. Still Coghlan presents the results in a manner as if we were dealing with the heritability of intelligence. We learn that "there is little dispute that genetics accounts for a large amount of

---

46 This refers to the fact that all molecular genetic studies so far had a negative result, i. e. did not find more than a minimal relation between SNP sequences and intelligence.

variation in people's intelligence," quite as if the heated debate about the validity of quantitative genetic data had never happened. The effect found, a *reduction* in intelligence as a consequence of the mutation, is presented to us as "... the best evidence yet that a single gene can raise IQ...," which is obviously supposed to let us think that we were dealing with a normal population in which people with a specific gene variant (in fact all people who do *not* have the mutation) are somewhat smarter than the others. Seen in this way, the mutated gene is the norm and the not mutated one is a variation of a normal gene which increases intelligence. According to this peculiar logic, the mutation found does not constitute a (mild) pathological state in which brain weight is reduced, but a gene finally identified as participating in the heritability of intelligence.

It is to be asked whether nonsense like this, quite like the nonsense of albinism as a pleiotropy, of phenylketonuria, or of the heritability of *change* of intelligence over the life span indicating the heritability of intelligence, is actually believed by the authors or whether we are dealing with conscious misinformation in the absence of valid molecular genetic evidence for the heritability of intelligence. Considering the improprieties the field has produced over more than 100 years, this question must be asked in earnest.

Summary and comment

Under normal scientific conditions, i.e. ones under which we can rely on a minimum of honesty in the presentation of data, this book could have been quite short, just as long as its first part. It is scientifically unequivocal that heritability coefficients are population specific to an extreme degree, that accordingly the estimates cover the whole range from 0.0 to 1.0, and that heritability coefficients practically do not tell anything about the malleability of mental capacity by means of social measures. This is obviously also the case for heritability values determined by molecular genetics for which, as mentioned, no evidence as to a substantial heritability of intelligence has been found yet, however. Population specificity and the mutual independence of heritability and malleability alone should suffice to terminate research in the field. What sense is there in heritability estimates if it is known in advance that, depending on environmental variability, nearly any values may result and that the coefficients do not allow us to determine the malleability of a trait, which would be the only discernable reason why they should be estimated in the first place.

Still, among a wider public and in broad areas of science, the impression prevails that the question about the heritability of intelligence is a reasonable one and that it already has been answered in favor of a high heritability of intelligence. In order to understand this discrepancy the second (and longer) part of the book has been added. It is supposed to show to what degree ideological and generally unscientific aspects, including plain incompetence (see Eysenck), have shaped the discussion. Science may never be immune to such effects but usually there are criteria for scientific truth which sooner or later make for a clear picture. In the field of research dealing with the heritability of intelligence this, at least so far, has not been the case. The situation here must be called chaotic in the sense that anyone who has a scientifically unsupported opinion about the topic may find a confirmation for it in the supposedly scientific literature, meaning that anyone may *even scientifically* think what he likes.

There are mainly two reasons for this situation. One emerges from the topic as such, the old question about the role of nature and nurture in shaping mental traits, a question which touches on fundamental convictions and the answer to which may be different depending on philosophical and, concomitantly, often on political convictions. Particularly since Jensen's 1969 article, it has been the intermingling of the question with political ideology (stressing the role of environment: politically left; stressing the role of the genes: politically right) which gave the debate its ardor and had the effect that scientific arguments were exchanged but seemingly, while in fact we were dealing with an ideological controversy which remained totally sterile scientifically.

There need not necessarily be an ideology behind the prescientific assumption of a high heritability of intelligence, however. The assumption that personality traits are heritable, quite like bodily ones, is probably as old as mankind. The belief in (ideology about) a dominance of the biological over the psychological and cultural has clearly reinforced it, supported in recent decades by the popular (and mostly wildly speculative) application of evolution theory to psychological and social problems in humans (see Velden, 2012). In an ideological climate like this, notions like the one about the high heritability of intelligence are not seen as prescientific any more and are therefore difficult to correct. Accordingly, such a correction therefore calls for particularly clear and strict scientific criteria which alone can force thinking to take a new direction.

With this we come to the second reason for the unsatisfactory situation of scientific offhandedness in the field, the repeatedly mentioned lack of such criteria. The extreme complexity of psychological traits and processes in general may preclude the unequivocal results typical of the natural sciences (there cannot be an exact, generally binding definition of intelligence, for example), but, with respect to the present topic, the observed general intellectual offhandedness has resulted in the actual possibility of an ultimate clarification of the problem not being used, perhaps not even seen. As we have seen this clarification actually cannot consist in a decision about a certain degree of heritability of intelligence (or just a certain range), but in the insight that on a-priori grounds there cannot be a specific degree of heritability of intelligence, that the question about the heritability may be intuitively plausible but actually makes no sense. This clearly results from a careful analysis of the meaning of the partitioning of the phenotypic variance (formula (4), p. 12) in combination with the definition of the heritability coefficient (formula (7), p. 16).[47] Such an analysis could have declared the project of determining the heritability of intelligence brain dead a long time ago, and much money, time and effort could thus have been saved.

The manifold misleading interpretations of data and facts, with the result that

---

[47] In addition, the essential independence of heritability and malleability, highly relevant in the context as we have seen, also follows from the definition of the heritability coefficient (see p. 19).

Summary and comment

the impression of a predominant genetic basis of mental traits and functions was upheld, have also contributed to the desolate state of the field. Whoever had hoped for an amelioration of the situation through molecular genetic studies has been disappointed. Even though the data entail no indication whatsoever as to a genetic basis of intelligence,[48] the impression is being upheld that there are clear indications for the heritability of intelligence, indeed that it is even a particularly high one (e.g. Plomin, 2012).

It may not be worthwhile to ask why the field of research about the heritability of intelligence suffers from such a degree of impropriety.[49] But it is utterly important to know *that* it does so suffer, because only against the background of this knowledge may the reader draw the only sensible conclusion, which is to study the methodological essentials and then to judge by himself. I hope that this book will encourage and help him to do this.

---

48 Less than 1 % of variance explained by genetic differences from unreplicated studies cannot be seen as such an indication.
49 The geneticist Richard Lewontin attested "carelessness, shabbiness and intellectual dishonesty" to the whole field (Lewontin, 1975, p. 402), a verdict which he today, 40 years later, would probably not revoke considering what I have described above.

Literature

Atkinson, R.L., Atkinson, R.C., Smith, E.E., & Bem, D.J. (1993). Introduction to Psychology (11th ed.). New York: Harcourt Brace Jovanovich College Publishers.
Bailey, R.C. (1997). Hereditarian scientific fallacies. *Genetica, 99,* 125–33.
Barnett, S.M., & Wiliams, W. (2004). National intelligence and the emperor's new clothes. *Contemporary Psychology, 49,* 386–96.
Bodmer, W.F. & Cavalli-Sforza, L.L. (1976). Genetics, evolution, and man. San Francisco: W.H. Freeman.
Booth-Kewley, S. & Friedman, H.S. (1987). Psychological predictors of heart disease: A quantitative review. *Psychological Bulletin, 101,* 343–62.
Brand, C. (1995). Burt-watching. *Nature, 377,* 394–5.
Brenton, D.P. (1996). Inborn errors of amino acid and organic acid metabolism. In D.J. Weatherall, J.G.G. Ledingham and D.A. Warrell (Eds.). Oxford Textbook of Medicine (3rd ed.), Vol. 2. Oxford: Oxford University Press. 1365.
Carlson, E.A. (2011). The Hoosier Connection: Compulsory Sterilization as Moral Hygiene. In P.A. Lombardo (Ed.), A Century of Eugenics in America. Bloomington: Indiana University Press. 11–25.
Coghlan, A. (2012). Single gene affects IQ – but only just. *New Scientist, 196,* No 2632, 16.
Cooper, R.M., & Zubek, J.P. (1958). Effects of enriched and restricted early environment on the learning ability of bright and dull rats. *Canadian Journal of Psychology, 2,* 159–64.
Darwin, C. (2004). The Descent of Man, and Selection in Relation to Sex (2nd ed.). London: Penguin. (First published in 1879 by John Murray, London).
Davenport, C. (1911). Heredity in Relation to Eugenics. New York: Henry Holt.
Deary, I.J. et al. (2012). Genetic contributions to stability and change in intelligence from childhood to old age. *Nature, 482,* No 7384, 212–5.
Ehrlich, P.R. (2000). Human Natures. Washington, D.C.: Island Press.
Eysenck, H.J. (1971). Race, Intelligence, and Education. London: Temple Smith.
Eysenck, H.J. (1973). The Inequality of Man. London: Temple Smith.
Eysenck, H.J. (1987). Rauchen und Gesundheit. Plädoyer für mehr Sachlichkeit. Düsseldorf: Rau.
Eysenck, H.J. (1998). Intelligence. New Brunswick: Transaction Publishers.
Falconer, D.S. & Mackay, T.F.C. (1996). Introduction to Quantitative Genetics (4th ed.). London: Longman.

Fisher, R.A. (1951). Limits to intensive production in animals. *British Agronomic Bulletin*, 4, 217–8.
Fisher, R.A. (1990). Quote. In Hirsch, J. (1990). A nemesis for heritability estimation. *Behavioral and Brain Sciences, 13(1)*, 137–8.
Fraser, S. (Ed.) (1995). The Bell Curve Wars. New York: Basic Books.
Galton, F. (1886). Regression towards mediocrity in hereditary stature. *The Journal of the Anthropological Institute of Great Britain and Ireland*, 15, 246–63.
Galton, F. (1869/1892). Hereditary Genius. London: Macmillan.
Gardner, H. (1983). Frames of mind: The theory of multiple intelligences. New York: Basic Books.
Goddard, H.H. (1928). Feeblemindedness: a question of definition. *Journal of Psychoasthenics*, 33, 219–27.
Hamer, D. (2004). The god gene: How faith is hardwired into our genes. New York: Doubleday.
Hamer, D., & Copeland, P. (1994). The science of desire: The search for the gay gene and the biology of behavior. New York: Doubleday.
Hebb, D.O. (1980). Essay on Mind. Hillsdale, N.J.: Lawrence Erlbaum.
Herrnstein, R.J., & Murray, C. (1994). The Bell Curve. New York: The Free Press.
Hirsch, J. (1990). A nemesis for heritability estimation. *Behavioral and Brain Sciences*, 13 (1), 137–8.
Hirsch, J. (1997). Some history of heredity-vs-environment, genetic inferiority at Harvard (?), and *The* (incredible) *Bell Curve*. *Genetica*, 99, 207–24.
Holmes, O.W. (1935). Quote in *Atlanta Constitution, March 9*, 1935.
Jensen, A.R. (1969). How much can we boost IQ and scholastic achievement? *Harvard Educational Review*, 39, 1–123.
Jensen, A. R. (1995). IQ and science: The mysterious Burt affair. In N.J. Mackintosh (Ed.), Cyril Burt – Fraud or Framed? Oxford: Oxford University Press.
Jensen, A. (1998). The g Factor. London: Praeger.
Kamin, L.J. (1974). The Science and Politics of IQ. New York: Lawrence Erlbaum.
Kempthorne, O. (1978). Logical, Epistemological and Statistical Aspects of Nature-Nurture Data Interpretation. *Biometrics*, 34, 1–23.
Kempthorne, O. (1997). Heritability: uses and abuses. *Genetica*, 99, 109–12.
Kitcher, P. (1996). The lives to come. London: Penguin Book Ltd.
Kosslyn, S.M., & Rosenberg, R.S. (2001). Psychology. Boston: Allyn and Bacon.
Kuhn, T.S. (1962). The Structure of Scientific Revolutions. Chicago: The University of Chicago Press.
Ladd-Taylor, M. (2011). Eugenics and Social Welfare in New Deal Minnesota. In P.A. Lombardo (Ed.), A Century of Eugenics in America. Bloomington: Indiana University Press.
Laughlin, H.H. (1924). Statement on March 8 to the Committee on Immigration and Naturalization, House of Representatives, 68th Congress, First Session, pp. 1231–1437 in U.S. House Hearings: Immigration, Serial 5 A. Washington Government Printing Office, Washington, D.C.
Layzer, D. (1974). Heritability Analysis of IQ Scores: Science and Numerology. *Science*, 183, 1259–66.

Lewontin, R.C. (1975). Genetic Aspects of Intelligence. *Annual Review of Genetics, 9,* 387 – 405.
Lewontin, R.C. (1995). Human Diversity. New York: Freeman.
Li, C.C. (1971). A tale of two thermos bottles: Properties of a genetic model for human intelligence. In R. Cancro (Ed.), Intelligence: Genetic and environmental influences. 162 – 81. Grune & Stratton.
Lombardo, P.A. (2011). Preface and Acknowledgments. In P.A. Lombardo (Ed.), A Century of Eugenics in America. Bloomington: Indiana University Press.
Mackintosh, N.J. (Ed.) (1995a). Cyril Burt – Fraud or Framed? Oxford: Oxford University Press.
Mackintosh, N.J. (1995b). Twins and other kinship studies. In N.J. Mackintosh (Ed.), Cyril Burt Fraud or Framed? Oxford: Oxford University Press.
Mackintosh, N.J. (1995c). Does it matter? The scientific and political impact of Burt's work. In N.J. Mackintosh (Ed.), Cyril Burt – Fraud or Framed? Oxford: Oxford University Press.
Murdoch, S. (2007). IQ – A Smart History of a Failed Idea. Hoboken, N.J.: John Wiley.
Myers, D.G. (2004). Psychology (7th ed.). New York: Worth Publishers.
Neisser, U. (2004). Serious scientists or disgusting racists? *Contemporary Psychology, 49,* 5 – 7.
Neisser, U., Boodoo, G., Bouchard, T.J., Boykin, A.W., Brody, N., Ceci, S.J., Halpern, D.F., Loehlin, J.C., Perloff, R., Sternberg, R.J., & Urbina, S. (1996). Intelligence: Knowns and Unknowns. *American Psychologist, 51,* 77 – 101.
Nisbett, R.E., Aronson, J., Blair, C., Dickens, W., Flynn, J., Halpern, D.F., & Turkheimer, E. (2012). Intelligence – New Findings and Developments. *American Psychologist, 6(2),* 130 – 59.
Platt, S.A., & Bach, M. (1997). Uses and misinterpretations of genetics in Psychology. *Genetica, 99,* 135 – 43.
Plomin, R. (2012). How intelligence changes with age. *Nature, 482, No.7384,* 165 – 6.
Plomin, R., DeFries, J.C. & McClearn, G.E. (1990). Behavioral Genetics (2nd ed.). New York: W.H. Freeman and Company.
Plomin, R., DeFries, J.C., Knopik, V.S., & Neiderhiser, J.M. (2012). Behavioral Genetics (6th ed.). New York: Worth Publishers.
Reuter, M., Roth, S., Holve, K. & Henning, J. (2006). Identification of first candidate genes for creativity: A pilot study. *Brain Research, 1069,* 190 – 7.
Reuter, M. (2007). Dopamin und positive Emotionalität. Presentation University of Mainz, May 5, 2007.
Richards, R.J. (1987). Darwin and the emergence of evolutionary theories of mind and behaviour. Chicago: The University of Chicago Press.
Rogers, A., & Jorde, L. (1995). Genetic evidence on modern human origins. *Human Biology, 67,* 1 – 36.
Rushton, J.P. (1988). Race differences in behaviour: A review and evolutionary analysis. *Personality and Individual Differences, 9,* 1009 – 24.
Samelson, F. (1996). He didn't? Yes, he did (probably)! *Contemporary Psychology, 41,* 1177 – 9.
Samelson, F. (1997). What about fraud charges in science; or, will the Burt Affair ever end? *Genetica, 99,* 145 – 51.

Sarrazin, T. (2010). Deutschland schafft sich ab. München: Deutsche Verlags Anstalt.
Savolainen, V., & Lehmann, L. (2007). Evolutionary biology: Genetics and bisexuality. *Nature, 445 (7124),* 158 – 9.
Scarr, S. (1974). Some myths about heritability and IQ. *Nature, 251,* 463 – 4.
Schönemann, P.H. (1997). On models and muddles of heritability. *Genetica, 99,* 97 – 108.
Schwarz, M., & Schwartz, J. (1973). Evidence against a genetical component to performance on IQ tests. *Nature, 248,* 84 – 7.
Shipman, P. (1994). The evolution of racism. New York: Simon & Schuster.
Tellegen, A., Lykken, D.T., Bouchard Jr., T.J., Wilcox, K.J., Segal, N.L., & Rich, S. (1988). Personality similarity in twins reared apart and together. *Journal of Personality and Social Psychology, 54,* 1031 – 9.
Terman, L.M., & Merrill, M.M. (1937). Measuring intelligence. A guide to the Administration of the new revised Stanford-Binet tests of intelligence. Boston: Houghton Mifflin.
Tucker, W.H. (2002). The funding of scientific racism. Urbana: University of Illinois Press.
Velden, M. (1997). The heritability of intelligence: Neither known nor unknown. *American Psychologist, 51,* 72 – 73.
Velden, M. (2003). The heritability of mental traits in humans: A proposal for a more coherent discussion. *Swiss Journal of Psychology, 62,* 5 – 10.
Velden, M. (2010). Biologism – The consequence of an illusion. Göttingen: V&Runipress.
Velden, M. (2012). Darwin's Shadow. Göttingen: V&Runipress.
Wahlsten, D. (1990). Insensitivity of the analysis of variance to heredity-environment interaction. *Behavioral and Brain Sciences, 13,* 109 – 61.
Wallace, A.R. (1869). Review of *Principles of Geology* by Charles Lyell, 10th ed., and *Elements of Geology* by Charles Lyell, 6th ed. *Quarterly Review, 126,* 359 – 94.
Watson, J.B. (1913). Psychology as the behaviorist views it. *Psychological Review, 20,* 158 – 77.
Yong, E. (2013). Chinese project probes the genetics of genius, *Nature, 497,* No 7449, 297 – 9.
Zimmer, C. (2008). The search for intelligence. *Scientific American, 299(4),* 52 – 59.
Zuckerman, M., & Brody, N. (1988). Oysters, rabbits and people: A critique of *Race Differences in Behavior* by J.P. Rushton. *Personality and Individual Differences, 9,* 1025 – 33.

Index

agronomy 9
albinism 53

behavioral genetics 7, 51
breeding, breeding success 7, 9, 18
Burt, C. 34–36

covariation (gene/environment) 12, 50

Darwin, C. 30, 39
Davenport, C. 30
DNA (desoxyribo nucleic acid) 7, 22

eleven plus (11$^+$) 34–38
eugenics 30–32
evolutionary psychology 40, 58
Eysenck, H. J. 44–51

factor analysis 34, 43
Falconer, D. S. 14, 15
feeblemindedness 31
Fisher, R. 14

Galton, F. 26–30
genotype/phenotype 10, 53
g factor 34, 35, 43
GODgene 51, 52

Hamer, D. 51, 52
Hebb, D. O. 10, 11
heritability coefficient
– generalizability, population specificity 15–18
– relation to malleability of a trait 18–21
– definition of 12, 16
– validity of 13–15
– objective of its determination 15, 18–21
Herrnstein, R. 32, 33
homo sapiens 16, 21
homosexuality (genetic basis of) 51, 52

immigration 32, 33
intelligence
– definition of 34
– and brain size 39, 41–43
– structure of 34, 43
– predictive power of 38
interaction
– definition of (statistical) 11
– gene/environment 11, 12, 48–51

Jensen, A. 40–44

Kamin, L. 35
Kitcher, P. 51

Lewontin, R. 43, 59

Mackintosh, N. J. 35, 36
Mankind Quarterly 51
molecular behavioral genetics
– and belief in God 51, 52
– and homosexuality 51, 52
– and intelligence 22–24

mutations (effects on mental traits) 53–56

natural science 7, 58
Neisser, U. 40, 51

phenotype/genotype 10, 53
phenotypic variation 10–12
phenylketonuria 54
Pioneer Fund 40, 44, 51
pleiotropy 53
Plomin, R. 22, 23, 53–55

quantitative genetics 9–21

race differences 39–43
racism 39–44

regression effect
– definition of 27–29
– with Eysenck 45–47
– with Galton 27–29
reification 43
Rushton, P. 40, 42, 44

Samelson, F. 36, 51
Sarrazin, T. 33
SNPs (single nucleotide polymorphisms) 22
Spearman, C. 34, 43
sterilization (compulsory) 31, 32

Tucker, W. H. 39, 44
twin studies 13–15